The Trail of Tears: The Relocation of the Cherokee Nation

Other titles in the American History series

The American Revolution
The Cold War
The Constitution and Founding of America
Environmentalism in America
The Industrial Revolution
The Salem Witch Trials
Twentieth-Century Immigration to the United States
Early Native North Americans

AMERICAN HISTORY

The Trail of Tears: The Relocation of the Cherokee Nation

Lydia Bjornlund

LUCENT BOOKS

A part of Gale, Cengage Learning

GALE
CENGAGE Learning

Detroit • New York • San Francisco • New Haven, Conn • Waterville, Maine • London

GALE
CENGAGE Learning™

LIBRARY OF CONGRESS CATALOGING-IN-PUBLICATION DATA

Bjornlund, Lydia D.
  The Trail of Tears : the relocation of the Cherokee Nation / by Lydia Bjornlund.
      p. cm. -- (American history)
  Includes bibliographical references and index.
  ISBN 978-1-4205-0211-4 (hardcover)
  1. Trail of Tears, 1838-1839--Juvenile literature. 2. Cherokee Indians--History--19th century--Juvenile literature. 3. Cherokee Indians--Relocation--Juvenile literature. 4. Indians of North America--Southern States--Relocation--Juvenile literature. I. Title.
    E99.C5B49 2010
    975.004'97557--dc22
                                                    2010001549

Lucent Books
27500 Drake Rd.
Farmington Hills, MI 48331

ISBN-13: 978-1-4205-0211-4
ISBN-10: 1-4205-0211-5

Printed in the United States of America
3 4 5 6 7 14 13 12

Contents

Foreword   7
Important Dates at the Time of the Trail of Tears   8

Introduction:
What Is the Trail of Tears?   10

Chapter One:
The Cherokees at Home   14

Chapter Two:
The Path Toward Removal   31

Chapter Three:
Moving Out   46

Chapter Four:
The Long Journey   60

Chapter Five:
Starting Over   76

Notes   93
For Further Research   96
Index   99
Picture Credits   103
About the Author   104

Foreword

The United States has existed as a nation for just over 200 years. By comparison, Rome existed as a nation-state for more than 1,000 years. Out of a few struggling British colonies, the United States developed relatively quickly into a world power whose policy decisions and culture have great influence on the world stage. What events and aspirations drove this young American nation to such great heights in such a short period of time? The answer lies in a close study of its varied and unique history. As James Baldwin once remarked, "American history is longer, larger, more various, more beautiful, and more terrible than anything anyone has ever said about it."

The basic facts of United States history—names, dates, places, battles, treaties, speeches, and acts of Congress—fill countless textbooks. These facts, though essential to a thorough understanding of world events, are rarely compelling for students. More compelling are the stories in history, the experience of history.

Titles in this series explore the history of the country and the experiences of Americans. What influences led the colonists to risk everything and break from Britain? Who was the driving force behind the Constitution? Which factors led thousands of people to leave their homelands and settle in the United States? Questions like these do not have simple answers; by discussing them, however, we can view the past as a more real, interesting, and accessible place.

Students will find excellent tools for research and investigation in every title. Lucent Books' American History series provides not only facts, but also the analysis and context necessary for insightful critical thinking about history and about current events. Fully cited quotations from historical figures, eyewitnesses, letters, speeches, and writings bring vibrancy and authority to the text. Annotated bibliographies allow students to evaluate and locate sources for further investigation. Sidebars highlight important and interesting figures, events, or related primary source excerpts. Timelines, maps, and full-color images add another dimension of accessibility to the stories being told.

It has been said the past has a history of repeating itself, for good and ill. In these pages, students will learn a bit about both and, perhaps, better understand their own place in this world.

1540
Hernando de Soto explores present-day Georgia; members of de Soto's party are probably the first Europeans to come into contact with the Cherokees.

1776
The Cherokees ally themselves with the Americans fighting the British during the American Revolution.

1827
The Cherokees draft a constitution, declaring themselves a nation.

1780–1820
The Cherokees sign treaties ceding portions of their land to the United States.

1830
Congress passes the Indian Removal Act.

1835
The Treaty of New Echota gives all of the Cherokee land east of the Mississippi River to the U.S. government.

1500	1600	1700	1800

1831
Nat Turner leads a slave revolt in Virginia, resulting in the deaths of about sixty white people.

1838
The Cherokees are forced off their land and begin the long walk westward along the Trail of Tears to new land in Indian Territory (now Oklahoma).

1861
The American Civil War is waged between the North and the South. Cherokees join the fighting on both sides.

1862
Congress passes the Homestead Act, opening western lands owned by Native American nations to white settlement and marking the beginning of mass migrations to Indian lands in the west.

1849
Gold is discovered in California, spurring the California Gold Rush, bringing thousands of settlers westward through Native American lands and disrupting the way of life for local groups.

Time of the Trail of Tears

1871
Congress passes the Indian Appropriation Act, disclaiming the sovereignty of Native American nations. The act determines that Indian policies will be established by acts of Congress or executive order rather than through treaties with Native Americans.

1876
George Armstrong Custer and 210 men under his command are killed during the Battle of the Little Bighorn.

1887
The Dawes Severalty Act eliminates common ownership of land by Native American nations. Native American land is broken into 160-acre (65ha) tracts allotted to Native American families and 80 acres (32ha) for individuals. The "surplus" land on reservations is opened up to settlement.

1900

2000

2010

1988
Congress passes the Indian Gaming Regulatory Act, affirming the right of Native Americans to allow gambling on their lands and paving the way for a new source of income from casinos.

1890
Congress establishes the Oklahoma Territory on "unoccupied" lands in the Indian Territory, breaking its promise to the Cherokees and other nations living there to preserve this area for the Native Americans forced from their lands in the east.

1898
The Curtis Act prohibits tribal governments from refusing land allotments and mandates that tribal lands in Indian Territory—including land belonging to the Cherokees—be allotted to individuals.

1924
Congress passes the Indian Citizenship Act, granting U.S. citizenship to Native Americans living within U.S. borders.

1942
World War II breaks out. During the course of the war, about twenty-five thousand Native Americans serve in the armed forces and another forty thousand are employed in wartime industries.

What Is the Trail of Tears?

In the summer of 1838, U.S. Army troops invaded land where the Cherokees had lived for generations. The people were forced from their homes and sent to government camps, where they awaited their departure to new land that had been set aside for them in present-day Oklahoma. These people had lived in peace.

The Cherokees loved the land on which they lived. As waves of white settlers moved into the woods of the southeastern states, they fought to protect their homes and villages. They signed treaties with U.S. commissioners, giving up some of their land in exchange for promises that they could live peacefully on the land that remained. The promises proved empty.

Contact and Conflict

By the 1820s an increasing number of white settlers were living illegally on land owned by the Cherokee Nation—a trend made worse after gold was discovered on Cherokee land in 1828. State governments ignored the Cherokees' petition for help to remove the settlers—in fact, most states put additional pressure on the Cherokees to leave. Their fate was all but sealed when Congress passed the Indian Removal Act in 1830. This act, pushed through Congress by President Andrew Jackson, set aside land in Indian Territory (present-day Oklahoma) for Native Americans in exchange for their land in the east. The law required all Native Americans to move west of the Mississippi River within five years of its passage.

Still, the Cherokees refused to believe the U.S. government would ignore its promises. They pointed to past treaties, which had been signed in good faith. Cherokee delegations went to Washington, D.C., to plead their case before Congress. They dined with U.S. presidents and cabinet members to request exemption from the Indian Removal Act. They pleaded their case in the Supreme Court.

For years, the Cherokees believed that justice would prevail.

The Place Where They Cried

The Cherokees' faith in the U.S. government proved unfounded. In 1838 the U.S. Army was ordered to evacuate all Cherokees from their homes and lead them westward to their new land in Indian Territory. They were forced from their homes and moved into hastily constructed forts. Crowded together in unsanitary conditions, the Cherokees became susceptible to diseases that swept through the forts. Hundreds died before they even started their westward journey.

To get to the land set aside for them, Cherokee men, women, and children walked 800 to 1,000 miles (1,200 to 1,600km), a journey that took up to six months. The Cherokee people suffered greatly along the way. Boats capsized. Wagons broke down. Food was scarce and spoiled. Death was common. Some Cherokees turned back, but most had no choice but to continue on, desperately hoping to reach their destination. In one group only 489 of an estimated 800 who set out together arrived in Indian Territory. One Georgia volunteer who took part in the removal later wrote, "I fought through the Civil War and have seen men shot to pieces and slaughtered by thousands, but the Cherokee removal was the cruelest work I ever knew."[1]

Although records of how many died are incomplete, historians estimate that at least four thousand of the sixteen thousand Cherokees who were living in the southeastern United States lost their lives in just one year.

Some historians, however, believe that the impact was much greater, particularly when taking into account the number of children who would have been born during the late 1830s had removal not occurred. One scholar, who undertook an analysis of the population figures, concludes that "a total mortality

A statue in Oklahoma City, Oklahoma, commemorates the Trail of Tears, the harsh journey thousands of Native Americans endured as they were forcibly removed from their homelands and relocated west of the Mississippi River.

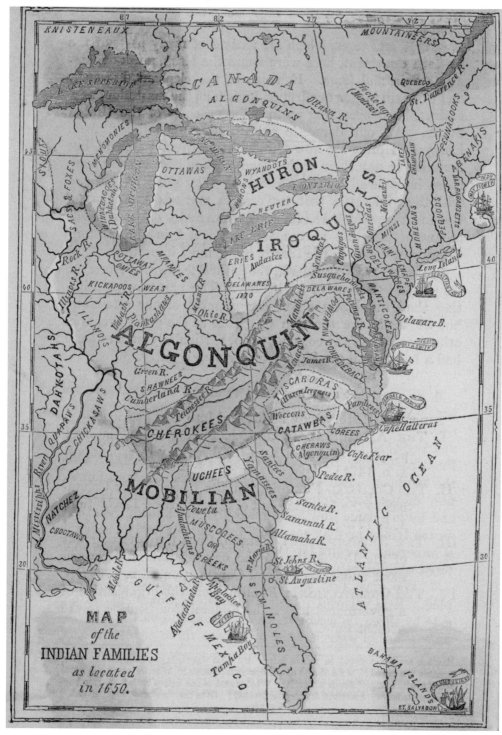

This map shows the locations of many Native American tribes in the mid-1600s, in what is now the eastern United States. During the 1700s and 1800s, many groups of native peoples, in addition to the Cherokees, were forced from their homelands by white settlers.

figure of 8,000 for the Trail of Tears period, twice the supposed 4,000, may not be at all unreasonable."[2]

Cherokees today still call the routes they took westward *nuna dat shun'yi*, which means "the place where they cried." The removal of the Cherokees and the various routes they took westward have become more commonly known as the Trail of Tears.

A Broader View

Unfortunately, the Cherokees' experience was not unusual. They were not the only group to travel hundreds of miles from their homeland to Oklahoma: the Choctaw, Chickasaw, Creek, and Seminole nations also marched across the southeast to new land in Indian Territory. Many historians include these nations in their accounts of the Trail of Tears. Other Native Americans living in other parts of the emerging United States experienced their own tearful trails, as they too were forced from their homelands.

The United States is not unique in its treatment of indigenous—or native—people. Throughout history and across the globe, people have been pushed off their land by more powerful groups. In some places, indigenous people have been assimilated into the new culture, often as slaves or laborers. In others, they have been wiped out entirely, intentionally by war or unintentionally through disease and famine. Sometimes, like the Cherokees, they have been forced to move. Even today, in some parts of the world, people are forced to flee to safer havens because someone more powerful wants their land or its resources. Also common today is the discord between two different cultures— two different ways of life—that results in ongoing conflict.

Strictly defined, the Trail of Tears is the main route or routes that the Cherokees took from the Southeast to the land the U.S. government identified as their new home in Indian Territory. But the Trail of Tears is not just a place: It has come to mean the journey itself—the experience of a people. The term defines the forced movement of a people and the immense sadness they felt. It is a tragic event—a time in history—caused by prejudice and greed. The Trail of Tears is a travesty of the democratic ideals on which our nation was founded.

Chapter One

The Cherokees at Home

Long before Spanish explorers first came to the North American coast in search of gold, the Cherokees roamed the mountains and forests of what is today the southeastern part of the United States. During their heyday, the Cherokees were the largest and most powerful tribe in the southeast. One historian estimates that as many as fifty thousand Cherokees lived during the mid-seventeenth century. In all, more than 140,000 square miles (362,600 sq. km) were once contained within the Cherokee Nation. The Cherokees lived in present-day Georgia, Tennessee, North and South Carolina, and Alabama. The state of Tennessee was named after the first Cherokee capital, Tanasi.

Cherokee comes from a Creek word, *Chelokee,* meaning "people of a different speech." Most Cherokees called themselves *Ani Yunwiya,* which means "the principal people," or *Keetoowah,* which means "people of Kituhwa," believed to

be one of the first large Cherokee villages.

The first contact between the Cherokees and Europeans occurred in 1540, when Hernando de Soto led an expedition of Spaniards in search of gold. The explorers met a group of Cherokees living near the Blue Ridge mountains. The Cherokees gave the expedition corn, turkey, and other food as well as a bison skin, which the soldiers described as "an ox hide as thin as a calf's skin, and the hair like a soft wool between the coarse and fine wool of sheep."[3]

Daily Life

The Cherokees lived for many generations before white men came to their lands, however. Like other Native Americans, they adapted to their surroundings in the foods they ate and the homes in which they lived. The Cherokees had two types of houses: large, rectangular houses with wooden sides and roofs for the summer months, and small, round houses that provided warmth in the winter. The winter houses, called *asi*, had a framework of large poles interwoven with branches. Walls were filled in with thick mud. At the center of each *asi* was a fire pit that provided warmth. In addition to these houses, outbuildings stored corn and other crops to last through the winter.

The Cherokee homesteads were clustered together in villages. Most villages consisted of about fifty families. Each village had a building where meetings could be held. This council house, which was a circular structure with thick mud walls, was essentially a much larger version of the *asi*. The council house had to be large enough to hold several hundred people because the entire village met there for ceremonies or to decide important issues.

The family was the core of Cherokee life. Extended family members—grandparents, aunts, uncles, and cousins—lived in the same village, and often in the same house, until separated by marriage. Cherokee families were divided into seven clans, which were essentially larger groups of more distant relatives. Each

The first contact between the Cherokees and Europeans occurred in 1540, when Hernando de Soto (center) led an expedition of Spaniards in search of gold.

A home similar to this was built by many Native Americans to shelter them during the winter months.

clan claimed an animal or other feature as its name and symbol. The Cherokee clans were Bird, Blue, Deer, Long Hair, Paint, Wild Potato, and Wolf.

The Cherokees used a matrilineal system—based on the mother's side of the family—to trace their descent. At birth, a Cherokee baby became a member of his or her mother's clan. The clan served as an extended family. A Cherokee traveling far from home could expect to receive food and shelter from his or her clan in other villages.

If a Cherokee woman married a white settler, her children were considered Cherokee. They became part of her clan.

An example of an early Native American village, with many homes clustered together and crops nearby.

As such intermarriages became common, the Cherokee Nation passed a law giving Cherokee citizenship also to the children of white women married to Cherokees. As a result, by the time of the Trail of Tears, the Cherokee Nation included hundreds of descendants of white settlers in their numbers. In some communities, Cherokees who had some white blood—were of mixed race—outnumbered full-blooded Cherokees.

It did not matter how many white ancestors a Cherokee had; anyone with Cherokee blood was a Cherokee in the eyes of both the Cherokees and the U.S. government. Mixed-race Cherokees lived in Cherokee villages and participated fully in Cherokee life. They learned the customs and habits of the Cherokees. "All it took was a drop or two of Cherokee blood to be considered Cherokee," writes one descendant. "Some say that Cherokee is not a matter of blood at all, but *a thing of spirit*."[4]

Life in the Village

The Cherokees were an agricultural people. Their primary crops were corn, beans, and squash. The fields used to grow these crops were not owned by individuals or families; rather, the women of a village would work together on communal farms. Women and children also foraged in nearby forests for wild berries, nuts, and fruits to supplement their diet. The plants

DARLEY.

Cherokee men were hunters, providing their families with meat, fish, and animal skins for clothing and tools.

provided not only food but also medicines to treat a wide variety of illnesses.

Men and women had different roles and responsibilities. Whereas the women tended the fields and took care of their children, the men were hunters and warriors. They often left for months at a time on the hunt for deer, wild turkeys, bears, and other animals. The meat from these animals was an important part of the Cherokee diet. The skins were used for clothing and tools. As the areas near Cherokee lands became settled by English colonists, the Cherokees also traded the skins for European tools and later for guns and ammunition. The Cherokee men also fished in rivers and streams with spears and nets.

An equally important role for men was warfare. The Cherokees traded with their Native American neighbors, but they also fought with them. War was routine, particularly among groups competing for the same hunting grounds. Encounters in the hunting grounds often resulted in casualties. The Cherokees believed that it was important to maintain balance in the world. If a member of the tribe was killed, the only way to restore balance was to avenge his or her death by taking the life of someone in the offending group. This responsibility fell to

Sequoyah and the Cherokee Alphabet

Sequoyah was born in 1776 in Tuskegee, Tennessee, to the daughter of a Cherokee chief. His father was Nathaniel Gist, a fur trader from Virginia. In addition to his Cherokee name of Sequoyah (which means "Pig's Foot"), Sequoyah was given the "white" name of George Gist.

Like most Cherokees of mixed blood, Sequoyah was raised as a Cherokee, steeped in Cherokee customs and traditions. As a young man, he became a silversmith. In this trade, he dealt regularly with whites and became fascinated by what Native Americans called their "talking leaves"—written papers and documents. Some historians say that Sequoyah began puzzling about how to write the Cherokee language when a white customer suggested Sequoyah sign his name on his works of silver. Others argue that he began his writing system to pass the time after a hunting accident. Although no one knows for sure what inspired him, historians agree that it took him years to develop his syllabary.

In Sequoyah's syllabary, symbols represent each of the distinct sounds in the Cherokee language. Because this invention allowed the Cherokees to keep diaries, write letters, and publish a national newspaper, historians have a wealth of information about the Cherokees' nineteenth-century experiences.

the clan. If a member of the Bear clan was killed by a Creek warrior, for instance, the Bear clan would have to revenge the death by killing a Creek. Of course, this would create an imbalance in the minds of the Creeks, who more likely than not would avenge this death with yet another. To early Europeans, this appeared to be a vicious cycle of violence.

Government

The Cherokee government, which was based on the clan system, also differed from the European model. Clans would make sure that a person was duly punished. Historians Theda Perdue and Michael D. Green write, "The obligations of clan members were so strong and so scrupulously fulfilled that the Cherokee had no need for a police force or court system: Protection, restitution, and retribution came from the clan."[5]

To address issues that affected the entire village, each village had a council made up of one elder from each clan. Only men served on the councils, but older women often earned significant respect from younger villagers. Decisions were made by consensus. All members of the council were welcome to give opinions and argue their point of view. "This does not mean that the Cherokee considered all people to be equal," write Perdue and Green. "Leadership in a Cherokee community, in fact, rested with a person who could inspire followers rather than in someone born to office."[6]

In addition to the village government, representatives from the villages met to decide issues of importance to all Cherokees. By the early 1800s, the Cherokee Nation was an established system of representative government. Numbering between sixteen and seventeen thousand people, the Cherokees were the most populous nation in the southeast. They also had a force of roughly six thousand warriors, making them one of the most powerful nations as well.

Trade

Warfare and politics were not the only reasons the Cherokees left their villages. The hunt for food often took Cherokee men many miles from their homes. Cherokees also traveled along waterways and footpaths to trade with other Native American groups living in the southeastern United States. Soon after the arrival of Europeans, the Cherokee Nation began to trade with them as well. Early on, the Cherokees traded beaded goods for woolen blankets and coats; later traders exchanged deerskins for a variety of European goods, including metal farm implements and other tools as well as guns and ammunition.

Trade with the Europeans forever changed the nature of life for the Native Americans. Many tribes soon became dependent on trade with the white man, craving metal axes, hoes, knives, and firearms. As explained in *Through Indian Eyes:*

As the people grew accustomed to metal tools, they lost the arts of chipping flint into arrowheads and shaping pieces of bone into knives and scrapers. As a result, foreign-made articles that began as luxuries were soon necessities. Without metal farm tools, Native American villagers could not raise enough food to sustain themselves. They were growing dependent on the white trades for their very survival.[7]

Disease Decimates Native Populations

European traders brought more than items to be traded: They also brought diseases. Smallpox, measles, and other diseases spread rapidly through Cherokee villages. The Native Americans had never been exposed to these European diseases and had no immunity to them. In addition, the Native American medicine men did not know how to treat the new diseases. Within just a few decades, diseases killed thousands of Cherokees. In some areas, entire communities were wiped out within just a few years of the first contact with Europeans.

In 1738 a smallpox epidemic spread rapidly through Cherokee villages. Some historians estimate that the Cherokee Nation lost as much as half of its population within a year. James Adair, an English trader who lived among the Cherokees for forty years, reported that some of the Cherokees committed suicide rather than suffer the disfigurement of the disease:

Native Americans, who once only traded goods with other native groups, soon took a great interest in trading goods with white settlers.

"Some shot themselves, others cut their throats, some stabbed themselves with knives and others with sharp-pointed canes; many threw themselves with sullen madness into the fire and there slowly expired, as if they had been utterly divested of the native power of feeling pain."[8]

War and Conflict

From the beginning, the colonial governments sought alliances with Native American groups, not only for trade but also in warfare. The colonies often took advantage of age-old rivalries to drive Native Americans off their land. In 1711, for instance, the Cherokee Nation and several other tribes joined the colonists in a war against the Tuscarora tribe in present-day North and South Carolina. The Tuscaroras had already been devastated by conflict and disease. Only about five thousand of the twenty-five thousand Tuscaroras who had lived prior to European contact remained. In what became known as the Tuscarora War—which raged for two years—thousands of Tuscaroras were killed or captured. Many of the prisoners—most of them women and children—were sold into slavery. In the peace treaty, the Tuscarora tribe ceded much of its land in North and South Carolina to the colonies. The majority of the remaining Tuscaroras moved north to take refuge among the Iroquois tribe, distant relatives in northern New York and Canada.

In exchange for their alliance with the colonies, the Cherokees received a promise of peace as well as a large stash of guns and ammunition. In 1721 the Cherokee Nation signed another treaty with South Carolina, establishing a fixed boundary between Cherokee land and the colony. Through such wars and skirmishes, Native American groups throughout the colonies were forced off their land. This was the first land cession made by the Cherokees to the Europeans.

Native Americans also became involved in ongoing conflicts between European groups in the New World. In general, the French fur traders and colonists tended to treat Native Americans better than the English did. As a result, Native American tribes tended to side with the French when conflicts broke out. The British colonists feared an alliance between France and strong Native American groups such as the Cherokee tribe. In 1730 Sir Alexander Cuming, a Scottish nobleman, visited Cherokee towns and met with their chiefs to win their friendship. He convinced several prominent chiefs and their councils to declare their allegiance to the king of England. When he returned to England, he was accompanied by seven Cherokee representatives, who met with King George II.

During their visit to England, the seven Cherokees signed a treaty again pledging their allegiance to and alliance with Britain. The treaty declared that any enemies of the English were the enemies of the Cherokees. It further decreed that the Cherokees treat the English as their own brothers and be prepared to fight against anyone who opposes them.

In 1730 Sir Alexander Cuming, center, met with several Cherokee chiefs with the goal of strengthening the allegiance between the Cherokee Nation and England.

The French and Indian War

When war broke out between the French and the British in 1754, the Cherokee Nation formally allied with the British, but many warriors fought alongside the French. In the colonies, this conflict became known as the French and Indian War.

The French and Indian War had a devastating effect on the Native Americans who lived in its path. Most Native American nations fought alongside their Eu-ropean allies, often engaging in more dangerous missions than their European counterparts. Thousands died fighting on one side or the other. Entire villages moved westward to get away from the conflict.

The Cherokees were among the many groups that also lost land due to the war. On February 10, 1763, the French and the British declared a truce with the Treaty of Paris. England emerged as the decisive victor, and France ceded all disputed

Britain emerged victorious from the French and Indian War. As a result, many Native American tribes that sided with the French lost land to the British as part of the peace treaty signed between Britain and France.

land claims. During the war, the Cherokee Nation had shifted its professed alliance from Britain to France. Thus, it was considered a defeated power in the peace treaty. Britain claimed Cherokee land as part of the treaty it signed with France.

For many native populations, the elimination of French power in North America also meant the loss of France as an ally that balanced England's power and curbed unchecked expansion into native lands.

The Gradual Loss of Land

In subsequent years, the Cherokees and other Native Americans in the southeast-

ern United States signed a series of treaties. The treaties were signed in good faith, but with heavy hearts. "Every treaty was essentially forced upon the Cherokee," writes one historian, "and only signed because they were assured that no further cessions would be demanded."[9]

Native American leaders believed that signing a treaty—even if it meant giving away some of their land—was the only way to form a permanent border that would protect the remaining land from the encroachment of whites. The treaties were largely useless, however. Even where colonial governments tried to enforce the treaties, white settlers simply ignored them and built homes and farms on the land that had been identified as belonging to the Cherokee tribe. White settlers raised local militia to protect them against Cherokee raids. Recognizing that they were outnumbered and outgunned, the Cherokee leaders signed yet another treaty ceding the now-occupied land in exchange for the promise to honor the new boundary.

In early treaties, the Cherokees ceded their hunting grounds. In 1776, however, conflict between whites and Cherokees resulted in the devastation of more than fifty Cherokee towns. In the quest for peace, the Cherokees signed a treaty giving up land in North Carolina. This marked the first time the land ceded included areas where towns and villages existed, some of which had been home to the Cherokee people for centuries.

The Cherokee also sometimes ignored the treaties. In the Henderson Purchase of 1775, for instance, the Native Americans ceded lands north of the Cumberland River and included most of what is now Kentucky. A loosely affiliated group of Cherokees, called the Chickamaugas, refused to honor the treaty; over the next several decades the Chickamaugas continually raided English settlements. This further angered white settlers, who rarely differentiated between different Native American tribes. An increasing number of settlers believed that the only way to protect themselves from such attacks was to remove the Native Americans from the land altogether.

A Proclamation in Defense of the Cherokees

Early presidents intended to honor their treaties with the Cherokees and the Cherokees' claim on their land. Responding to reports of anarchy and deaths of Cherokees along the borders between white settlements and Cherokee lands, President George Washington warned that those who broke the law would be brought to justice. In 1792 Washington signed a proclamation declaring that such "outrageous conduct not only violates the rights of humanity, but also endangers the public peace." Washington argued that the honor of the nation depended on pursuing all legal means for the apprehension and punishment of the offenders. The government also offered a five-hundred-dollar reward to U.S. citizens and officers who brought the offenders to justice.

Quoted in John Ehle, *The Trail of Tears: The Rise and Fall of the Cherokee Nation*. New York: Anchor, 1988, p. 42.

The *Cherokee Phoenix*

One of the many achievements of the Cherokee Nation was the *Cherokee Phoenix*, the first Native American newspaper. Headquartered in the Cherokee capital of New Echota, the first issue rolled off a new printing press on February 28, 1828. Recognizing that the Cherokees were not the only Native Americans who were in need of support, the name of the newspaper was changed in 1829 to the *Cherokee Phoenix and Indian Advocate*.

For the next seven years—until the Cherokees were forced from their homes on the Trail of Tears—the *Cherokee Phoenix* served as the official voice of the Cherokee Nation. Articles were published in both Cherokee and English. The newspaper was used to print new laws and meeting notices as well as to bring together the far-flung Cherokees as one nation, united in their defense of their homeland, values, and customs.

The Impact of the American Revolution

The Cherokees began to blame the settlers—not the British government—for the ongoing loss of their land. Thus, when war broke out between the American colonists and Great Britain, many Cherokees sided with Great Britain. Colonists fighting for Britain—called Loyalists—got help from Cherokee villages, and Cherokee warriors joined British troops. The southern colonies struck back. South Carolina offered a bounty for the scalps of Cherokee warriors. Throughout the southern colonies, troops raided Cherokee villages, burning their houses and fields. By the end of the war, the American colonists had destroyed more than fifty towns and left the Cherokee people at great risk of starvation.

In 1783 representatives from England and the new United States signed a treaty to end the Revolutionary War. In the treaty, England ceded all of its land in North America to the United States. The territory of the Cherokee Nation, like that of other Native American groups, was included in this land. One of the first challenges for U.S. leaders was to decide how to deal with this land and the indigenous people who lived on it. Among the issues to be decided was what level of government—state or national—had the authority and responsibility to deal with the Indians.

In 1783 both North Carolina and Georgia granted Cherokee lands to their citizens. The Cherokees vehemently protested, claiming that the states had no right to give their land to anyone. Although most Cherokees sought to resolve the dispute peacefully, the Chickamaugas took up arms against the white settlers who encroached on their land and the militia who sought to protect these settlers.

The new federal government sought to put an end to the conflict between states and Native Americans. In 1785 commissioners from the U.S. government met with Cherokees at Hopewell, South Carolina. The resulting Treaty of Hopewell defined the boundaries of Cherokee territory and recognized the right of the Cherokee Nation to expel whites who tried to settle on its land. The treaty accomplished little, however. Both Georgia and North Carolina refused to recognize the treaty, saying that Congress had no right to interfere in the states' relationships with the Native Americans within their borders. Tensions between the federal government and the southern states would continue for decades, with the Cherokee people caught in the middle.

A New Nation's Policy and Promises

The U.S. Constitution, which was ratified in 1789, gave authority over "Indian affairs" to the federal government. The next year Congress passed a law requiring all purchases of Native American land to be made by treaties between tribal leaders and commissioners appointed by the U.S. government. Federal lawmakers hoped that this would avoid conflict between states and the U.S. government and reduce the risk that agreements with Native Americans would make conflicting promises.

In conjunction with Secretary of War Henry Knox, who was responsible for Indian affairs, President George Washington crafted a policy for dealing with Native American groups. Knox complained about the "disgraceful violation of the treaty of Hopewell with the Cherokee" and was critical "of the lawless whites" who ignored the boundaries spelled out in that treaty.[10] Knox favored putting soldiers within Cherokee territory to protect the Indians against the encroachment of whites.

Washington and Knox believed that the best solution was for the Cherokees to assimilate into white culture. Essentially, assimilation is a process in which one group—in this case, the Native Americans—assumes the customs and beliefs of another—in this case, white Americans.

Part of Washington's strategy involved making peace with Native American tribes. In 1791 the U.S. government signed a treaty that guaranteed the Cherokee Nation 70,000 square miles (181,300 sq. km) of territory. This land lay within the states of Georgia, North Carolina, South Carolina, and what would become Alabama, Kentucky, and Tennessee. One of the goals of the 1791 Treaty of Holston was "that the Cherokee nation may be led to a greater degree of civilization and become herdsmen and cultivators instead of remaining in a state of hunters."[11] To this end, the United States agreed to furnish the Cherokee people with farm implements, tools, and draft animals as well as people to demonstrate their use. In her book *The Trail of Tears Across Missouri*, Joan Gilbert describes the exchange: "The Cherokee gave up large parts of their hunting grounds in the treaty, but they were promised some advantages; in exchange for the land, the treaty promised them peace, the protection of the federal government, an annual payment, and tools useful for farming."[12]

Assimilation was not new, and it was perhaps a more obtainable aim for the Cherokees than for any other Native American group. From the earliest contact with Europeans, the Cherokees had adopted many of the ways of their white neighbors. Whites married into the Cherokee Nation, and Cherokees moved off traditional lands into log cabins and brick mansions. An increasing number of Cherokees wore European-style clothing and practiced Christianity. This process increased after the American Revolution, as the federal government believed that assimilation would enable Native Americans and whites to live in harmony.

Chapter Two

The Path Toward Removal

From the beginning, Native Americans were viewed as a serious threat to the colonies and then the new United States. Negotiating and dealing with Native American nations were important government responsibilities. The United States ultimately negotiated, signed, and ratified almost 390 treaties with Native American groups. These treaties were formal government-to-government negotiations regarding the exchange or sale of land and property rights owned by Native American groups. The treaties recognized the Native American tribes as independent and sovereign entities that could negotiate as equals with the United States.

The drafters of the U.S. Constitution were concerned about securing the nation's power to make binding agreements with the Native Americans. They feared state interference. Because Native American nations did not fall neatly within one state, having different states negotiate their own independent treaties to set boundaries could result in conflict and confusion. In the Constitution, which went into effect in 1789, the framers gave sole authority over Indian affairs to Congress and the president.

In essence, the framers of the U.S. Constitution considered the Native American tribes to be much like other nations. They considered the Indians to be sovereign entities—with the right to govern themselves. Just as the leaders of the United States did not want one state to be able to sign treaties with England, France, or any other foreign nation, so too they believed that states should be prohibited from negotiating with Native Americans. In 1790 Congress passed the Indian Trade and Intercourse Act. This law required that all purchases of land from Indians must be arranged through treaties negotiated by tribal leaders and representatives appointed by the president.

Cherokee Alphabet

(Chart of Cherokee syllabary characters arranged in rows and columns)

Sounds represented by vowels.

a as a in *father* or short as a in *rival*
e as a in *hate* or short as e in *met*
i as i in *pique* or short as i in *pit*
o as aw in *law* or short as o in *not*
u as oo in *fool* or short as u in *pull*
v as u in *but*, nasalized

Consonant Sounds.

g nearly as in English, but approaching to k. d nearly as in English but approaching to t. h, k, l, m, n, q, s, t, w, y as in English. Syllables beginning with g except g have sometimes the power of k, a, e, o, u are sometimes sounded to, tu, tv, and syllables written with tl except tl sometimes vary to dl.

In addition to learning how to read and write their own language, the development of the Cherokee alphabet allowed Cherokees to establish a written constitution.

living among them boasted that the literacy rate among Cherokees—that is, the number of people who could read—was higher than among their white neighbors. Perhaps more than any other Native American nation, the Cherokee people assumed the ways of whites, earning them the moniker "the civilized tribe."

The Cherokee people also learned to read and write English, but there was no written alphabet for the Cherokee language—or for any Native American tongue. In the early 1800s a Cherokee named Sequoyah began to work on a system of writing the Cherokee language. Sequoyah, the son of a Cherokee mother and an English father, was a silversmith. His work brought him in close contact with whites who had settled in the area. He believed that writing would help his people advance in the white man's world, and he began working out a writing system. In 1821 Sequoyah introduced his system of syllabary for the Cherokee language. The syllabary worked like an alphabet, but each of the eighty-six characters represented a different speech sound in the Cherokee language. This made it relatively easy for Cherokees to quickly learn to read and write in their own language.

Soon after the introduction of Sequoyah's system, the Cherokee Nation began publication of the *Cherokee Phoenix*, which printed articles in both English and Cherokee. From its inception in 1828 until it was forced to close in 1834 due to lack of funds, the *Cherokee Phoenix* (later called the *Cherokee Phoenix and Indian Advocate*) provided a critical means for the Cherokee people to share news and voice opinions. Sequoyah's syllabary also made it possible for the Cherokee to adopt a written constitution, which it based on the Constitution of the United States.

Racism and Reactions

Despite the Cherokee Nation's strides toward assimilation, many Americans remained skeptical of the tribe. They believed that Native Americans were an inferior race. One Georgian in Congress referred to the Cherokee people as "savages" who lived on "roots, wild herbs [and] disgusting reptiles."[13]

In addition, many whites were frightened of the "savage" natives. Their fears were enhanced by graphic stories of Native American raids on villages. They heard about the kidnapping of women and children and the scalping of men. Not surprisingly, they did not want any of these Native Americans to live where they planned to build their homes and raise their families.

Meanwhile, the population of the United States soared. White settlers continued to encroach on Cherokee lands, clearing woods and building homesteads on land the Cherokees had been promised. Throughout the South, cotton plantations were springing up, bringing riches to those who had land and slave labor. Would-be plantation owners looked for fertile land, putting increasing pressure on the Native Americans who lived there. Southerners grew increasingly impatient with the federal government's promises to resolve the problem through peaceful negotiation. They believed assimilation was impossible. U.S. leaders hoped that the Native Americans living east of the Mississippi River would agree to exchange their land for new land in the west. Some groups did so and left peacefully to join distant relatives elsewhere, but many tribes put up a fight. Andrew Jackson, a Tennessean who served as a general in the army, was among the many people who believed the best

The Cherokee Phoenix *was published from 1828 to 1834.*

The Cherokee Constitution

In 1827 the Cherokees adopted a written constitution. Like the U.S. Constitution, it included a preamble that spelled out its aims:

We the Representatives of the people of the Cherokee Nation, in Convention assembled in order to establish justice, ensure tranquility, promote our common welfare, and secure to ourselves and our posterity the blessings of liberty, acknowledging with humility and gratitude the goodness of the sovereign ruler of the Universe affording us an opportunity so favorable to the design and imploring his aid and direction in its accomplishments do ordain and establish this Constitution for the Government of the Cherokee Nation.

Quoted in Carole Bucy, "Cherokee Constitution," History 2020—American History, Volunteer State Community College. www2.volstate.edu/cbucy/History%202030/Documents/Cherokee%20Constitution-Doc52.htm.

way to remove the Indians from the land was by force.

The U.S. Army often formed alliances with one Native American group against a rival tribe. For many generations, the Native American groups in the southeast had fought over territory and hunting grounds, so they often saw the expulsion of neighboring tribes as advantageous. Perhaps too the Cherokee Nation saw the United States as a powerful ally. Thus, when U.S. troops fought to push out the Creek tribe in 1814, Cherokee warriors joined Jackson's troops.

Over the next decade, the Native American tribes in the southeastern United States signed a series of treaties. Most of these treaties offered an end to the fighting if the Native Americans agreed to cede their land to the U.S. government. Treaties with the Cherokee Nation in 1817 and 1819, the Choctaw tribe in 1820, and the Creek tribe in 1826 all contained provisions to encourage groups to move west. This offer was formally endorsed with the Indian Removal Act of 1830, in which the federal government set aside land west of the Mississippi River—in an unsettled area that would become Indian Territory and then the state of Oklahoma—in exchange for Indian land in the southeast. By way of the treaties, the United States gained control over three-quarters of Alabama and Florida as well as parts of Georgia, Tennessee, Mississippi, Kentucky, and North Carolina.

Faced with constant hostility and pressure from whites, many Native Americans saw moving as their only option. They could leave freely and take what the government had to offer, or they would be forced out and left with nothing. In 1810 about eight hundred Cherokees moved to present-day Arkansas. In an 1816 treaty, another four thousand Cherokees gave up their land in Tennessee in exchange for land in northwestern Arkansas. In addition, the United States promised to pay the Cherokee Nation sixty thousand dollars: annual payments of six thousand dollars over ten years. Over the ensuing years, other Cherokees would join their western brethren. By 1820 more than six thousand Cherokees were living west of the Mississippi.

Most Cherokees had no interest in leaving their homeland, however. The leaders of the Cherokee people in the southeast believed they had already lost too much of their land to whites and took measures to protect the land that remained. This was complicated by the fact that ownership of the land was not always clear. Prior to white settlements, the Cherokees did not use ownership deeds showing who owned what parcel. Cherokee leaders realized that they needed to make sure that both Native American and white leaders knew who had the power to make treaties. In 1817 the Cherokee Nation passed a law giving its leaders—the National, or Cherokee, Council the sole authority to sell land. Individual Cherokees were prohibited from selling their houses and barns. In 1829 the Cherokee Council strengthened its power by making violation of this law punishable by death.

The Cherokee Constitution

The Cherokee Nation also strengthened its national government. In 1827 Cherokee delegates met at New Echota, Georgia, to draft a written constitution. The resulting document revealed many of the ways in which the Cherokees had adopted the ways of the whites. Much of the Cherokee constitution mirrored the constitutions of the United States and the state governments. For instance, the Cherokee government was divided into three "distinct departments: the Legislative, the Executive, and the Judicial."[14] The constitution divided the Cherokee

When the Cherokee Nation drafted a written constitution in 1827, the document, among other things, clearly outlined the boundaries of Cherokee land.

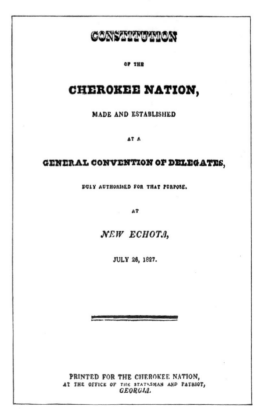

Nation into eight districts and gave all male members over eighteen years of age the right to vote. In August 1828 Cherokee voters elected John Ross as their principal chief.

The stated purpose of the Cherokee constitution was "to establish justice, ensure tranquility, promote our common welfare, and secure to ourselves and our posterity the blessings of liberty."[15] A primary concern of those writing the constitution was to ensure the authority of the Cherokee Nation. The Cherokee constitution was careful to delineate the boundaries of Cherokee land. It declared that all land within these boundaries belonged to the Cherokee Nation in common—not to individuals. The constitution also declared that the Cherokee people living within these boundaries were subject only to the laws of the Cherokee Nation.

Many Americans saw the Cherokee constitution as proof that the Cherokees could become—and were becoming—assimilated. This was the first time that a Native American group had written a constitution to govern itself. But many others did not like what the constitution said. The governor of Georgia especially was angry about the Cherokee Nation's claim to be a sovereign nation—its claim that the Cherokees were not subject to the laws of Georgia or the United States. State officials believed they had the right to enforce Georgia's laws on the land the Cherokee people claimed was theirs.

Tensions Mount

As more and more whites moved onto the land claimed by the Cherokees, tensions mounted. In 1829 gold was found on Cherokee land in the northwestern part of Georgia, near what is today Dahlonega. Rumors of gold spread quickly, and white settlers rushed into Cherokee lands to make their claims. Mining operations soon sprang up, attracting more gold miners. Within a year more than four thousand people were working the Georgia mines, which were producing over 300 ounces (8,505g) of gold a day. In the face of such riches, the gold miners cared little that they were trespassing on Cherokee land.

Georgia became increasingly aggressive in pushing the Cherokees off their land. Georgia officials argued that they had a right to establish and enforce laws governing Native Americans within their borders. In 1828 the state passed laws stripping the Cherokees of their rights. According to state laws, the Cherokees had no right to sue whites or testify in court. This made it impossible for Cherokees to defend their claims on their land.

The Cherokees fought to protect their land from white encroachment. In January 1830, for instance, the Cherokee Nation sought and obtained permission from the U.S. government to force whites off Cherokee land. About eighteen families had settled at Beaver Creek, about 30 miles (48km) southwest of present-day Rome, Georgia. Major Ridge, a Cherokee leader who had fought alongside Andrew Jackson, led about thirty young Cherokee braves to the area, where they destroyed the settlement and led the whites off the land. The Cherokees had acted within their legal rights

When gold was discovered in 1829 on Cherokee land in the northwestern part of Georgia, thousands of white settlers flocked to mine the area, with no regard that they were trespassing on Cherokee land.

and no one was hurt, but the eviction infuriated Georgia's leaders and frightened its citizens. Pressure to remove the Native Americans mounted.

Recognizing that they would get no help from the states, John Ross and a group of Cherokee representatives traveled to Washington, D.C., to ask for help from Congress. The delegation asked that the federal government honor its treaties with the Cherokees and enforce the boundaries between Georgia and the Cherokee Nation. Most members of Congress were indifferent to the plight of the Cherokees, but a few argued that the United States should keep its promises. In the Senate, Daniel Webster and Henry Clay argued before Congress that removal was unconstitutional and unwarranted. Davy Crockett, a U.S. representative from Tennessee, also defended the Cherokees, despite the fact that the people in his home state were strong supporters of removal. Historians believe that Crockett's defense of the Indians cost him his political career.

The Indian Removal Act

The plight of the Cherokees and other Native Americans was all but sealed when Andrew Jackson became president in 1828. Jackson was a forceful proponent of Indian removal. In his first address to Congress, Jackson said the Native Americans were "surrounded by the whites with their arts of civilization, which by destroying the resources of the savage doom him to weakness and decay." White encroachment forced the Native Americans farther into the wilderness, Jackson contended, "keeping them in a wandering state" that made any attempt at civilizing the Indians impossible.[16]

Jackson also did not consider the Native American tribes to be independent nations. He thought it was absurd for the U.S. government to enter into negotiations and treaties with Native Americans. If tribes within the U.S. boundaries refused to sell their land, the government should simply take it. In exchange, the

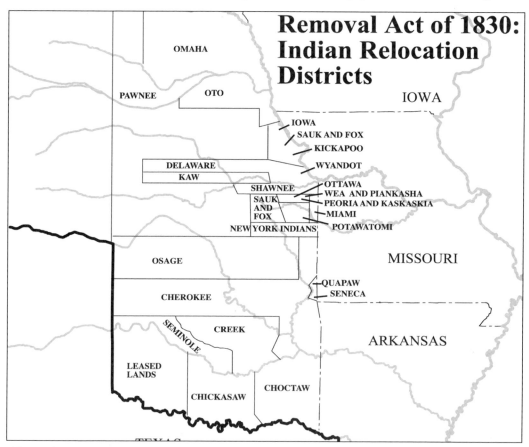

Removal Act of 1830: Indian Relocation Districts

Shown here is the new land that tribes would receive in exchange for giving up their land in the east.

President Jackson's Indian Policy

In the following excerpt from his 1830 annual address, Jackson explains how the Native Americans would benefit from the Indian Removal Act.

The consequences of a speedy removal will be important to the United States, to individual States, and to the Indians themselves. . . . It will separate the Indians from immediate contact with settlements of whites; free them from the power of the States; enable them to pursue happiness in their own way and under their own rude institutions; will retard the progress of decay, which is lessening their numbers, and perhaps cause them gradually, under the protection of the Government and through the influence of good counsels, to cast off their savage habits and become an interesting, civilized, and Christian community. . . .

Toward the aborigines of the country no one can indulge a more friendly feeling than myself, or would go further in attempting to reclaim them from their wandering habits and make them a happy, prosperous people. . . . Rightly considered, the policy of the General Government toward the red man is not only liberal, but generous.

Quoted in James D. Richardson, ed., *A Compilation of the Messages and Papers of the Presidents.* New York: Bureau of National Literature, 1897, pp. 1083–86. http://lincoln.lib.niu.edu/all.html.

government should offer them land west of the Mississippi, free from white interference. He argued that this would benefit not only the whites who desired to settle on Native American lands but also the Indians themselves. Within a year of taking office, Jackson pushed a new piece of legislation, called the Indian Removal Act, through Congress. The act gave the president the power to negotiate removal treaties by which tribes would give up their lands east of the Mississippi in exchange for lands to the west. Jackson believed that it was necessary to separate the Native Americans from the Europeans who were settling along the East Coast. "No state could achieve proper culture, civilization, and progress, as long as Indians remained within its boundaries,"[17] he wrote on signing the act. Any Native Americans who did choose to remain would become citizens of their home states, subject to state laws.

In his 1830 State of the Union address, Jackson called the Indian Removal Act a "benevolent policy." He added, "We now propose to acquire the countries occupied by the red men of the South and West by a fair exchange, and, at the expense of the United States, to send them to a land where their existence may be prolonged and perhaps made perpetual."[18]

Over the next several years, the War Department set about carrying out Jackson's removal plan. During Jackson's administration, the War Department negotiated seventy treaties with Native American groups. In many cases, the treaties were negotiated with a faction of a tribe, not with the chiefs elected by the entire nation. Most of the treaties included provisions in which Native American groups ceded land in the eastern United States in exchange for other land west of the Mississippi. By 1837—the end of Jackson's second term in office—more than forty-five thousand Native Americans had been removed from the east through this process.

On to the Supreme Court

The Cherokee Nation continued to look for help from the U.S. government. With Congress no longer seen as an ally, the Cherokees took their complaint to the Supreme Court. In *Cherokee Nation v. Georgia*, which reached the Supreme Court in 1831, the Cherokee Nation sought to stop the state of Georgia from enforcing state laws on Cherokee land. Supreme Court Justice John Marshall wrote that Georgia's laws were "alleged [to] go directly to annihilate [wipe out] the Cherokee as a political society, and to seize for the use of Georgia, the lands of the nation which have been assured to them by the United States, in solemn treaties repeatedly made and still in force."[19]

Much to the dismay of the Cherokee Nation, the Supreme Court refused to hear the case. The Court argued that, because the Cherokee people lived within U.S. territory, they were a "dependent" nation. The U.S. Constitution allowed only sovereign and independent nations to sue state governments. Although the federal government had always treated the Cherokee Nation as a sovereign nation, the Supreme Court did not believe that American Indian nations had the same rights as other sovereign nations such as France or England. The Supreme Court denied the Cherokees the right to sue the government.

Just a year later, another case involving Cherokee authority was brought before the Supreme Court. *Worcester v. State of Georgia* was brought on behalf of two white missionaries living among the Cherokees. Georgia state law required missionaries to obtain a license to live with and minister to Cherokees. Several missionaries believed that the state of Georgia would deny them a license because they supported the Cherokees in their fight against removal. Georgia learned that missionaries were living among the Cherokees with no license and ordered them to leave the state. The missionaries refused to do so. Seven missionaries were arrested, convicted, and sentenced to four years of hard labor.

In 1832 the Supreme Court heard the case of *Worcester v. State of Georgia*. (Samuel Austin Worcester was one of the missionaries.) The lawyer defending the missionaries argued that the state of Georgia had no authority over what happened on Cherokee land. The lawsuit contended that the land on which the Cherokees lived was not part of Georgia. Georgia could no more make laws

THE CASE

OF

THE CHEROKEE NATION

against

THE STATE OF GEORGIA:

ARGUED AND DETERMINED AT

THE SUPREME COURT OF THE UNITED STATES,

JANUARY TERM 1831.

WITH

AN APPENDIX,

Containing the Opinion of Chancellor Kent on the Case ; the Treaties between
the United States and the Cherokee Indians ; the Act of Congress of
1802, entitled ' An Act to regulate intercourse with the Indian
tribes, &c.'; and the Laws of Georgia relative to the
country occupied by the Cherokee Indians,
within the boundary of that State.

BY RICHARD PETERS,

COUNSELLOR AT LAW.

Philadelphia:

JOHN GRIGG, 9 NORTH FOURTH STREET.

1831.

The Cherokee Nation sought to stop Georgia from enforcing state laws on Cherokee land in Cherokee Nation v. Georgia, *which reached the Supreme Court in 1831.*

governing what people did within the Cherokee Nation than they could governing what people did in North or South Carolina. The law requiring missionaries to have a license was unconstitutional.

This time the Supreme Court ruled in favor of the Cherokees. In the decision, Justice Marshall said that the U.S. Constitution gave authority in Indian affairs to the national government, not state governments. The Court agreed that Georgia could not impose laws in Cherokee territory.

"Build a Fire Under Them"

In the end, the Supreme Court's ruling made no difference. In a famous quotation, President Jackson allegedly said, "John Marshall made his decision; now let him enforce it!" Some historians say Jackson probably never spoke these exact words, but they sum up his actions and his attitude. The federal government under Jackson did nothing to stop Georgia or its citizens from seizing Cherokee land and continuing to harass the Cherokee people when they protested.

Georgia also had grown impatient with the federal government's promise to obtain Cherokee land within the state. In 1832 Georgia held two land lotteries that divided the Cherokee land into 160-acre (65ha) lots. In this lottery system, which had been used in other parts of the state, Georgia residents could enter their name to win the right to buy a lot for four dollars. The winners of the lottery were supposed to wait for the Cherokees to leave before taking ownership, but many moved onto the land right away. Some winners of the lottery sold their right to the land to others. Many of the buyers believed that the deed gave them legal ownership of the land, regardless of the Cherokees' claims. The Cherokees disagreed. They became increasingly angry about the influx of squatters on their land.

The Cherokees' Objections

The Cherokee Nation petitioned the United States to be exempt from the Indian Removal Act. The following excerpt is from an 1830 address written from the council of the Cherokee Nation to the people of the United States.

We are aware, that some persons suppose it will be for our advantage to remove beyond the Mississippi. We think otherwise. Our people universally think otherwise. . . .

We wish to remain on the land of our fathers. We have a perfect and original right to remain without interruption or molestation. The treaties with us, and laws of the United States made in pursuance of treaties, guaranty our residence, and our privileges and secure us against intruders. Our only request is, that these treaties may be fulfilled, and these laws executed.

[If] we are compelled to leave our country, we see nothing but ruin before us. The country west of the Arkansas territory is unknown to us. . . . [It] is not the land of our birth, nor of our affections. It contains neither the scenes of our childhood, nor the graves of our fathers.

Quoted in Jennifer Erbach, "The Cherokee Removal: Group D Readings," Abraham Lincoln Historical Digitalization Project, 2002. http://lincoln.lib.niu.edu/teachers/lesson5-groupd.html.

President Jackson continued to support the right of the state to claim the land. He believed the best solution was for the Cherokees to leave the land voluntarily, and he thought that pestering Cherokee residents might be the best way to persuade them to do so. "Build a fire under them," Jackson advised. "When it gets hot enough, they'll go."[20]

When white settlers and speculators realized that no one was going to stop them from seizing land, many more moved to Cherokee land and stepped up their harassment to get the Cherokees to leave. White settlers cut wood on Cherokee property, harvested their crops, and mined the gold found on Cherokee land. Some vandalized stores owned by Cherokees and stole horses or other property. Those who had purchased land in the lottery began to build homes and clear the land, even though the Cherokees still claimed title to the land. Some Georgians took over the homes where Cherokee families were already living.

In 1833 John Ross went to Washington, D.C., to file suit against those who threatened to take over his property only to return to find whites living in his home, operating his farm, and running his ferry.

His wife and children had been forced out and were living with friends nearby. Ross had no choice but to join them.

Peace and Prosperity

The Cherokee Nation had always sought a peaceful solution. It had petitioned Congress and the Supreme Court. Although these attempts failed, John Ross and other Cherokee leaders continued to write letters to friends and Congress and go to Washington to plead their case. Elias Boudinot, the editor of the *Cherokee Phoenix*, wrote a series of editorials against removal, uniting the Cherokees and gaining new support among non-Cherokee people. Many whites spoke out in defense of the Cherokees, too. Women's groups and missionaries took up their cause, circulating petitions and writing letters of protest.

The Cherokee Nation continued to govern despite an 1830 law passed by Georgia. The law made it illegal for the Cherokee government to meet unless its purpose was to plan for removal. Anyone speaking out against removal was subject to arrest. The law also required whites living in the Cherokee Nation to declare allegiance to the state. A special police force was formed to enforce Georgia's laws within Cherokee territory. In response, the Cherokee council decided that the government should be moved beyond the reach of Georgia. The Cherokee leaders chose Red Clay, Tennessee, as the new government site. Red Clay was within the Cherokee Nation's boundaries and just across the border of Georgia. It served as the site of the Cherokee government from 1832 until 1837.

Meanwhile, the Cherokee people continued to farm and run their businesses. They believed that the best way to prove they could live in peace was to continue to turn a blind eye to the wrongs they suffered at the hands of whites. They counted many whites among their tribe—those who had married into the Cherokee Nation numbered in the hundreds. There were also many missionaries who lived among the Cherokees and counted them as friends. The Cherokee Nation pleaded with the white government and the white community for understanding and empathy.

Many Cherokees believed that they would prevail in the end—that the United States would live up to the promises it had made and allow them to live on their land. But as the 1830s wore on, an increasing number of Cherokees began to believe that they were fighting a losing cause.

Chapter Three

Moving Out

Many of the Native Americans living along the East Coast believed that the only way to stop the erosion of their land and the constant conflict with whites was to move west. As early as 1794, the first trickle of Cherokees left their ancestral homeland to flee the encroachment of white settlers. These Cherokees settled in southeastern Missouri, but they soon moved again, settling farther west between the White and Arkansas rivers in what is now Arkansas. They received title to this land in a treaty signed on July 17, 1817. In this treaty, the Cherokees ceded land of equal size east of the Mississippi River.

Over the next couple of decades, several hundred more Cherokees took advantage of the government's offer of free land in the west and joined their tribespeople in Arkansas. The Cherokees soon learned that they had not gone far enough west, however. Once again the rush of settlers in quest of land led to conflict. On May 6, 1828, the western Cherokees ceded their land in Arkansas in exchange for new land in so-called Indian Territory. The western Cherokees have since called this area home—the eastern part of present-day Oklahoma. Over the next decade, these "Old Settlers" would be joined by thousands of others. By the early 1830s, more than four thousand Cherokees were living west of the Mississippi River.

A Schism in the Cherokee Nation

Many of these early movers left their homes reluctantly. Some believed that they could find a better way of life free of interference from the U.S. or state governments. Others believed that migration was inevitable. Perhaps still others looked forward to an opportunity to start anew.

Those who stayed behind were under increasing pressure to move. By the early 1830s this caused a rift among the Cherokee Nation in the eastern United States. A small but powerful faction had come to believe that the only way the nation could survive was to take the federal government's offer to exchange their land and move west. This faction became known as the Treaty Party.

The Treaty Party was led by some powerful and prominent Cherokees, including Major Ridge and his son, John; Elias Boudinot, the editor of the *Cherokee Phoenix*; and Andrew Ross, John Ross's brother. Many of these men were patriotic Cherokees who had fought

John Ross was elected as principal chief of the Cherokee Nation in 1828. He was firmly against any treaty that would forfeit Cherokee land to the U.S. government.

John Ross

When the Cherokee Nation was formed in 1828, John Ross was elected as its first principal leader. Ross held this position until his death in 1866. He led the fight against the removal of the Cherokees, tirelessly writing letters and editorials, meeting with leaders of the U.S. government to plead his case, and working with lawyers to bring suit against those who would trample the rights of the Cherokees.

Ross was only one-eighth Cherokee by blood, but he lived as a Cherokee for his entire life. Like many Cherokees, he adopted the ways of whites. Ross served as a lieutenant in the Creek War, siding with Andrew Jackson's troops to force out the Creeks. He also served as a translator for U.S. agents negotiating treaties with Native Americans and for the missionaries who settled in and around Cherokee land. By the time the Cherokees were forced from their land in 1838, Ross had become one of the richest men in northern Georgia. He had a 200-acre (81ha) farm and a ferry operation, and he owned several slaves.

Ross lost his fight to stay on Cherokee land in the east. His beloved wife, Quatie, was among the hundreds of people who died on the Trail of Tears.

After the Cherokees settled on their new land in Indian Territory, Ross successfully led the effort to unite the eastern and western bands of Cherokees and forge a new Cherokee Nation. Ross's leadership in forging a new government and community no doubt was a factor in the success of the Cherokees to rebuild their community.

hard to retain their native land. Major Ridge, for instance, was a full-blooded Cherokee (meaning all of his ancestors were Cherokees) who had earned respect as a noble warrior. He had championed education and civilization of the Cherokees and had sent his son, John, to the finest schools available to Cherokee people. But Ridge had come to believe that assimilation was an impossible dream. "There is but one path to safety," argued Ridge at the New Echota meeting, "[and] one road to future existence as a Nation."[21]

John Ross was among those who ar-gued against any treaty that would cede additional land to the United States. Ross had been elected as the leader of the Cherokee Nation. He was one-eighth Cherokee and seven-eighths white, but he and his followers thought of him as nothing but Cherokee. Ross's followers were convinced that he would be able to convince white leaders to leave the Cherokees on their native land.

The anti-treaty group—those who continued to argue against removal—became known as the National Party or, more commonly, as simply the Ross Party. This group of Cherokees wanted to fight for their land. They believed that the government could not force the Cherokee people to leave against their will.

The Treaty of New Echota

Conflict grew between the Treaty Party and the National Party. The two groups began vying for power. Each sent a delegation to Washington. Each held meetings with treaty commissioners.

In the fall of 1834 the two parties held separate councils. The Treaty Party drew up a resolution explaining its position on removal. Delegates expressed "the sorrowful conviction" that it was impossible to "live in peace and comfort" on their native lands. They spelled out their options as moving west "or sinking into a condition but little, if at all, better than slavery."[22]

The federal government pressed its advantage. In 1835 John F. Schermerhorn, a treaty commissioner, invited the Cherokees to New Echota to craft a treaty. An estimated two to three hundred of the roughly seventeen thousand members of the Cherokee Nation attended the meeting. On December 29, 1835, officials of the U.S. government and about twenty Cherokees settled on the terms of a removal treaty. The Cherokees did so despairingly. "I have just signed my death warrant,"[23] announced Major Ridge after signing the treaty.

The Treaty of New Echota became the legal basis for the forcible removal of the Cherokee people. According to the provisions of the treaty, the Cherokee Nation ceded all of its lands east of the Mississippi River in exchange for equal

acreage in Indian Territory. The United States also agreed "to remove the Cherokee to their new homes and to subsist them one year after their arrival there."[24] The treaty further promised that each group of emigrants would be accompanied by "a sufficient number of steamboats and baggage-wagons" and "a physician well supplied with medicines."[25] The removal would take place

Major Ridge was one of the signers of the Treaty of New Echota, which called for the Cherokee Nation to cede all of its land east of the Mississippi River in exchange for equal amounts of land in Indian Territory.

Reasons for Signing the Treaty of New Echota

The delegates who signed the Treaty of New Echota were patriotic Cherokees who signed the treaty with heavy hearts. In the following excerpt, Major Ridge, one of the leaders of the Treaty Party, gives insight into why he believed the treaty was needed:

The Georgians have shown a grasping spirit lately; they have extended their laws, to which we are unaccustomed, which harass our braves and make the children suffer and cry. . . . The Indians have an older title than theirs. We obtained the land from the living God above. They got their title from the British. Yet they are strong and we are weak. We are few, they are many. We cannot remain here in safety and comfort.

We can never forget these homes, but an unbending, iron necessity tells us we must leave them. I would willingly die to preserve them, but any forcible effort to keep them will cost us our lands, our lives and the lives of our children. There is but one path to safety, one road to future existence as a Nation.

Quoted in Thurman Wilkins, *Cherokee Tragedy: The Ridge Family and the Decimation of a People*, Norman:, Oklahoma University Press, 1996, pp. 286–87.

within two years of Senate ratification. Families who did not wish to move could become citizens of their new state, with the notable exception of Georgia, which denied citizenship to anyone with Cherokee blood.

Protests

Unfortunately for the Cherokees, the tribe had no real way to decide the issue. The state of Georgia would not allow the Cherokees to assemble or hold elections. The *Cherokee Phoenix* ceased publication in 1834, and there were no real means for debate in other newspapers. As a result, many Cherokees knew little about the pros and cons of agree-ing to leave their land or what the alternatives might be.

As a result, both the signers of the treaty and those who were opposed to it claimed that they were the leaders of the Cherokee Nation and represented the wishes of the people. The drafters of the treaty claimed that the representatives at New Echota were "fully authorized and empowered . . . to enter into and conclude a treaty with the United States commissioner."[26]

John Ross and members of the National Party disagreed. None of the treaty signers was a chief or a member of the National Council. Moreover, in Ross's opinion, the Treaty Party had gone against the will of the people. Ross and his followers protested the authority of the delegates to enter into a treaty, the terms of the agreement, and the manner in which it had been negotiated.

In early 1836 protest meetings against the treaty were held throughout the Cherokee Nation. The next Red Clay Council meeting was attended by hundreds of Cherokees and lasted for three days. As a result of this meeting, a delegation was sent to Washington to formally protest the New Echota treaty. The treaty would not become law until it was ratified by the U.S. Senate, and Ross acted quickly to plead his case before Congress. In an impassioned letter to the U.S. Congress, he wrote:

> [The treaty] is not the act of our Nation; we are not parties to its covenants; it has not received the sanction of our people. The makers of it sustain no office nor appointment in our Nation, under the designation of Chiefs, Head men, or any other title, by which they hold, or could acquire, authority to assume the reins of Government, and to make bargain and sale of our rights, our possessions, and our common country.[27]

The debate in Congress was heated. Some legislators argued that the treaty was not drafted in good faith and that it went against previous promises of the government. But most legislators wanted an end to the so-called Indian problem. They wanted to carry out the terms of the

Indian Removal Act. On May 23, 1836, the Senate voted on the Treaty of New Echota. The treaty was ratified by just one vote.

For the next two years, Ross pleaded with the government to reverse its decision. He went to Washington to seek advice on how to overturn the treaty. He believed that the government officials would see that the treaty was illegal.

The Cherokee Council Meeting

During this time, Ross also called for a General Council of the Cherokees to discuss the Treaty of New Echota. In September 1836 an estimated three thousand Cherokees convened at the Red Clay Council Ground in Tennessee. Over the next three days, the council discussed the situation confronting the Cherokee Nation. Ross told the attendees that the treaty was illegal. He described the land that the U.S. government had set aside for the Cherokees as dry and uninhabitable. It was already occupied by other people. He believed the government would soon recognize the treaty as illegal and pleaded with the Cherokees to refuse to move off Cherokee land. At the end of the meeting, the Cherokees unanimously voted to reject the New Echota treaty.

Little gain was made in the next year or so. In the summer of 1837, the General Council met again. More than four thousand Cherokees attended the meetings. With the deadline for removal looming large, feelings ran higher than ever. Once again, the council ended with a vote of support for resisting removal. At the meeting, an eight-member delegation was appointed to proceed to Washington to argue on behalf of the Cherokee Nation. To prove that the treaty did not represent the will of the people, Ross and his supporters gathered signatures on a petition of protest. The petition was signed by 15,665 Cherokees. Ross personally delivered the petition to Congress in the spring of 1838.

Others came to the support of the Cherokee Nation. In an 1838 letter to President Martin Van Buren, poet Ralph Waldo Emerson called the plan for removal

> a dereliction of all faith and virtue, . . . a denial of justice, and . . . a deafness to screams for mercy … an act of fraud and robbery. . . . A crime is projected that confounds our understanding by its magnitude, a crime that really deprives us as well as the Cherokees of a country. . . . Will the American government steal? Will it lie? Will it kill?[28]

Getting Ready

Such pleas fell on deaf ears. President Van Buren, like Jackson, had come to believe that removing Native Americans from the eastern states was the best course of action. He defended the validity of the Treaty of New Echota and began to prepare for the exodus of the Cherokee people. This would be no easy task. An 1835 census conducted by the U.S. government counted 16,542 Cherokees living east of the Mississippi River. Just over three-quarters of these (77 per-

cent) were "full blooded," meaning that almost 25 percent had at least one white ancestor. The census also counted 201 whites who were married to Cherokees and 1,592 African slaves.

Government agents also began to value the land and the homes and farms that had been built on it. Worried that the Cherokees might stage an armed resistance, the federal government sent in troops to keep peace. General John E. Wool, who led the troops, was dismayed by the Cherokees' attitude. Clearly, this would be no voluntary removal. Most Cherokees were following Ross's orders to resist removal in any way possible. "It is vain to talk to a people almost universally opposed to the treaty and who maintain that they never made such a treaty," Wool wrote in an 1837 letter. "Many have said they will die before they leave the country."[29]

Wool pleaded with the Cherokees to leave voluntarily. He warned them that the U.S. government planned to enforce the terms of the Treaty of New Echota. If they did not leave voluntarily, they would be captured and forced to emigrate. The Cherokees who left before the deadline would benefit from the terms of the treaty, he said, but those who refused risked losing everything. He called the people who were encouraging them to stay on the land "the worst of enemies. Their advice, if followed, will lead to your certain destruction."[30]

Wool would not be part of this plan. He was willing to help those who enrolled for voluntary removal, but he did not want to force those who refused. He saw all that the Cherokee people were giving up in leaving behind their homes, farms, businesses, and many other possessions. "They are being robbed and plundered . . . subjected to every species of oppression," Wool complained. "Ninety-nine out of a hundred of them will go penniless to the West."[31] In 1838 he received his request for a transfer, and General Winfield Scott took over command of the Cherokee removal.

Meanwhile, many whites feared that the Cherokees would resort to war. The governor of Georgia claimed to have received a letter from a Cherokee who said that if the federal government would not cooperate, the Cherokees would rise up and join the Creek and Seminole tribes in a bloody war against the United States. Historians believe the letter was fabricated. Again and again, Cherokee leaders and the councils meeting at Red Clay committed to resolve the crisis without bloodshed.

The Rich Take Flight

Wool confirmed what the Treaty Party had been saying. Under attack from John Ross and his supporters, the signers of the Treaty of New Echota continued to defend their decisions. In 1837 Elias Boudinot published a pamphlet defending the actions of the Treaty Party. Boudinot was well educated and had been the editor of the *Cherokee Phoenix* for many years. He explained that he signed the Treaty of New Echota because the Cherokees were left with no recourse. He pointed to the suffering of the Cherokee people and called their situation "wretched." Boudinot said he was among the many Cherokees who believed that removal was their only option. "Instead of contending uselessly against superior power, the only course left, was to yield to circumstances over which [the Cherokees] had no control," he wrote. "Removal is the only remedy, the only *practicable* remedy. By it there *may be* finally a renovation; our people may rise from their very ashes to become prosperous and happy, and a credit to our race."[32]

Over the next two years, hundreds of families left their homes and joined the Old Settlers in the West. Among the first to leave were the signers of the Treaty of New Echota. Some historians believe that they were concerned for their safety amid the anger of their fellow Cherokees.

Most of the families who migrated in 1836 and 1837 were relatively prosperous. Their wealth helped to protect them from the hardships of the long journey. They traveled by wagon train and took horses and livestock with them. Like those who would come after them, they traveled on narrow roads across the primitive countryside. They slept in their wagons. Probably the greatest challenge—and the greatest risk—involved crossing rivers. The mighty Mississippi was especially formidable.

Captain B.B. Cannon, a member of the Tennessee Volunteer Infantry, led 365 Cherokees who chose to emigrate in the summer of 1837. The government paid for this group to move west. Cannon's group followed trade roads through Tennessee, Kentucky, Illinois, Missouri, and

The forced removal of the Cherokee people from their homeland to Indian Territory began in 1836.

Arkansas—traveling more than 800 miles (1,287km) in all. The route was carefully planned to pass through towns where the group could replenish supplies and make any needed repairs. It also passed near springs and waterways that would provide clean drinking water for people and animals.

In all, Cannon's journey took almost three months. Along the way, several other groups of Cherokee emigrants joined up with the travelers. Most of these early emigrants, who were wealthy and well equipped, made it to their new homes in Oklahoma. Cannon reported having to stop for several days because of illness; records suggest that 15 of the 365 travelers died on the journey. The death rate would be far higher among later groups.

The Summer of 1838

As May 1838—the deadline for removal—approached, only a couple of thousand Cherokees had adhered to the terms of the agreement. The government estimated that more than fifteen thousand remained.

Under the command of General Winfield Scott, the U.S. Army was charged with removing the remaining Cherokees from their homes. Scott issued the order:

> The commanding officer at every fort & open station will first cause to be surrounded and brought in as many

Indians, the nearest to his fort or station, as he may think he can secure at once, & repeat the operation until he shall have made as many prisoners as he is able to subsist and send off, under a proper escort, to the most convenient of the emigrating depots, the Cherokee Agency, Ross Landing, and Gunter's Landing. These operations will be again and again repeated . . . until the whole of the Indians shall have been collected for emigration.[33]

Scott wanted the removal to be "done judiciously, if possible, and, certainly, in mercy."[34] Many soldiers followed Scott's orders and treated the Cherokee people kindly. Scott later wrote that the roundup went well in most areas.

In Georgia, however, the removal was off to a bad start. In that state, the two thousand troops under Scott's command were assisted by the Georgia Guard, an often-brutal force that cared little for the Cherokees or their needs. Scott later recalled, "The great difficulty was with the Georgians (more than half the army), between whom and the Cherokees there had been feuds and wars for many generations. The reciprocal hatred of the two races was probably never surpassed. Almost every Georgian, on leaving home . . . vowed never to return without having killed at least one Indian."[35]

Evan Jones, a missionary who lived among the Cherokees, wrote in his diary, "The work of war in time of peace is commenced in the Georgia part of the Cherokee nation, and is carried on, in

In 1838 General Winfield Scott was put in charge of the U.S. Army's operation to relocate all remaining Cherokees to Indian Territory.

most cases, in the most unfeeling and brutal manner; no regard being paid to the orders of the commanding General, in regard to humane treatment of the Indians."[36] At one plantation, the Georgia Guard threw a burning log into the hallway to smoke the people out of their home. At another, family members were driven from their home as they prepared for the funeral of a child who had died the previous night.

The soldiers caught many families off guard. Held at gunpoint, they had little time to pack their things or prepare for the journey. Some were forced from their homes with nothing but the clothes on their backs. Following the troops were whites who scooped up the possessions that the Cherokees were unable to take with them. The soldiers objected, but they had their hands full moving the Cherokees and could do little to stop the looters.

A People Caught Unawares

It was cruel work. One soldier who participated in the removal later described the scene:

Men working in fields were arrested and driven into stockades. Women were dragged from their homes, by soldiers whose language they did not understand. Children were separated from their parents and driven into stockades with the sky for a blanket and the earth for a pillow. The old and infirm were prodded with bayonets to hasten them to the stockades.[37]

As the groups were rounded up, they were taken to forts, moving from one to another until they reached one of the three main depots: Old Agency on the Hiwassee River, near present-day Cal-

The Legend of Tsali

Tsali, or Charlie, lived outside the boundaries that the Cherokee Nation had established in its constitution. He was a traditionalist, a farmer who continued in the traditions of his ancestors. He cared little about the ways of whites and heard little news of the events leading up to the Trail of Tears.

Tsali was surprised when his brother-in-law warned him that soldiers were coming to take him and his family from their homes. He planned to escape to the mountains, but the troops arrived before he had a chance. Tsali and his family gathered a few meager belongings and followed the soldiers toward the stockade. Along the path, a soldier prodded Tsali's wife with his bayonet. Tsali was infuriated. He told his family in Cherokee that when he pretended to trip, they should grab the soldiers' guns. During the struggle, one of the guns went off, killing one of the soldiers. Tsali and his family fled into the hills.

The army was told to capture the murderers at any cost. Tsali, one of his sons, and his brother-in-law were executed by a firing squad. Rumors spread among the Cherokees that Tsali had turned himself in to the U.S. Army in exchange for a promise that the army would leave the other Cherokees living in the mountains alone. This legend—the belief that Tsali had sacrificed his life so his people could remain in their homeland—helped to fuel the resistance of the North Carolina Cherokees.

houn, Tennessee; Ross's Landing (Chattanooga, Tennessee); and Gunter's Landing (Guntersville, Alabama). Rich and poor, elderly and newborns, frail, ill, pregnant, and lame—all were forced into forts to await the journey west.

Jones, the missionary who worked among the Cherokees in North Carolina and accompanied them on their journey west, wrote on June 16 from a camp:

The Cherokee are nearly all prisoners. They have been dragged from their houses, and encamped at the forts and military posts, all over the nation. In Georgia, especially, multitudes were allowed no time to take anything with them, except the clothes they had on. Well-furnished houses were left a prey to plunderers, who, like hungry wolves, follow in the train of the captors. . . . Females, who have been habituated to comforts and comparative affluence, are driven on foot before the bayonets of brutal men. It is a painful sight.[38]

Some Cherokees voluntarily joined the groups, especially after it became clear that everyone was going to be forced to go. In a letter dated June 28, 1838, one soldier wrote that he alone accompanied nine hundred Cherokees from North Carolina to Fort Cass. "I arrived with about one hundred more than what I started with, many having joined me on the march," he wrote. "We were eight days in making the journey (80 miles [129km]) and it was pitiful to behold the women & children, who suffered exceedingly—as they were all obliged to walk, with the exception of the sick."[39]

The Forts

After being forced from their homes, the Cherokees were herded into stockades at Rattlesnake Springs near Chattanooga, Tennessee, where forts had been hastily constructed to house them. The camps grew to accommodate the thousands of Cherokees awaiting departure. At its largest, Fort Cass in Charleston, Tennessee, was 12 miles (19km) long and 4 miles (6.4km) wide.

On June 26, Winfield Scott wrote an upbeat letter to the U.S. secretary of war: "Families & individuals, with very few exceptions, have become cheerful. I have ordered all, who require it, to be vaccinated. The operation has commenced, & the supplies of every sort are abundant."[40] Yet it is hard to believe that the Cherokee people were as cheerful as this letter suggests. They had left behind everything they knew. Many were forced to leave with few possessions. No doubt they worried about neighbors, friends, and family who were in different camps. And none of them knew what awaited them on the other side of their journey.

Those Who Remained Behind

Most Cherokees surrendered to their fate, but not everyone was aware of what was happening. Many of these Cherokees were "traditionalists" who lived in North Carolina, outside the boundaries of the Cherokee Nation. The traditionalists did not adopt the ways of the whites; instead, they continued to hunt and farm in the traditional ways of their ancestors. They lived as their ancestors had and knew little about the Indian Removal Act or the Treaty of New Echota. When they heard that their brethren were being rounded up, hundreds fled to the nearby mountains and woods.

Over time, the army lost interest in the few Cherokees scattered in the woods. The army gave up pursuit in 1842, and the fugitive Cherokees were allowed to remain in an "unofficial" status. In 1848 Congress gave official recognition to the Eastern Band of Cherokees. Their descendants number more than eight thousand.

In addition to the Indians who hid from the army, another four hundred or so Cherokees remained behind because they were exempt from the army's order for removal. These Cherokees—members of a band known as the Qualia in North Carolina—had been granted U.S. citizenship and individual parcels of land in treaties in 1817 and 1819. Because they were no longer members of the Cherokee Nation, they were not subject to removal.

History suggests that these Cherokees who remained behind were the lucky ones. For the most part they were allowed to live much as they had in the past. Although they continued to face discrimination and hostility from their white neighbors, the Cherokees who stayed behind were spared the hardships of a 1,000-mile (1,609km) westward march.

Chapter Four

The Long Journey

The U.S. Army had experience in moving Indians. Many of the Native Americans who had called the eastern United States home had already been removed to lands in the west. The Cherokee were among the largest groups to be moved, however. Soldiers were to lead groups of several hundred Cherokee at a time. The initial plan was to have them travel by steamboat down the Tennessee and Ohio rivers to the Mississippi, where they would continue overland to Indian Territory. The army would leave several days between departures to allow the army to provide provisions at depots along the way.

The Cherokees Set Out

On June 6, 1838, the first detachment of Cherokees and their meager belongings were loaded onto long wooden flatboats of various sizes. Most of the boats had roofs over part of the hull, bunks inside for sleeping, and a small area for cook-

ing. Despite these amenities, the flatboats were crowded and uncomfortable. Roughly eight hundred Cherokees in all were in this first group, including the black slaves they owned. Most of them were from Georgia. They carried their few belongings. Two more groups soon followed, departing on June 15 and June 17. In all, these three groups included twenty-eight hundred Cherokees. Each group was accompanied by a U.S. military officer, a corps of assistance, and two physicians.

The flatboats were pulled by a series of steamboats on a circuitous river route along the Tennessee, Ohio, Mississippi, and Arkansas rivers. The rivers did not flow all the way to the Indian Territory. When they were no longer navigable, the Cherokees were herded into wagons and trains to continue the journey through Arkansas. Since there were not enough wagons for everyone, the Cherokees who were healthy had to walk.

The trip took a heavy toll. The summer of 1838 was hot. Some of the boats got stuck on sandbars. The Cherokees often had to move from boats that were no longer useful onto other boats, resulting in dangerously overcrowded conditions. In one expedition, 311 people died when a loaded flatboat capsized. Sickness and death were daily reminders of the perils of the trip.

The official reports of the soldiers who accompanied the expeditions and letters to loved ones at home tell of the hardships the Cherokees endured on their journey. One private later recalled:

On the morning of November the 17th we encountered a terrific sleet and snow storm with freezing temperatures and from that day until

The approximately three-months-long journey to the Indian Territory was rough and often dangerous. Sickness, hunger, and death were common among the Cherokees being moved.

we reached the end of the fateful journey on March the 26th 1839, the sufferings of the Cherokee were awful. The trail of the exiles was a trail of death. They had to sleep in the wagons and on the ground without fire. And I have known as many as twenty-two of them to die in one night of pneumonia due to ill treatment, cold and exposure.[41]

Historians are not sure exactly how many Cherokees lost their lives, but they estimate that as many as 25 percent of the Cherokees on the first expeditions died of disease, hunger, and exposure to the cold. In one of the early groups, just 602 of the 875 who had set out from Tennessee arrived at their final destination. In another, just 489 of the initial 800 arrived. Some of the Cherokees escaped and made their way back to the east. Rumors of the meager rations, rotten food, and harsh conditions frightened those who awaited passage.

On June 19 General Scott ordered the forced emigrations to be suspended until September 1. Scott planned to follow his orders to evacuate the Cherokees, but he was alarmed by the problems faced by the first groups. "His objective of a fast and efficient, yet compassionate, military operation had proven impossible," writes one historian. "It was severely handicapped by the weather and the obstinacy of the Cherokee, who were putting up passive resistance by deserting and by refusing to accept supplies and to properly muster."[42]

Scott hoped that waiting until autumn might help remedy some of the problems the early contingents had encountered. Fall rains would result in a higher water level in the rivers, making the rivers and waterways more navigable. There would be less risk of having boats get stuck on sandbars. He also hoped that sickness would not spread as quickly in cooler weather.

Taking Control

Disheartened by the turn of events, the Cherokee Council sent a letter to General Scott requesting that the Cherokee people be allowed to plan and lead their own removal. General Scott agreed to the Cherokees' request to organize the remainder of the removal operation.

The Cherokees elected John Ross and six others as the removal committee. Ross divided the Cherokees into thirteen detachments, ranging in size from about seven hundred to more than two thousand. The military was to provide wagons and horses or mules to pull them, but Ross arranged for the groups to go overland so they could hunt along the way. Those who had money could also buy food and supplies to supplement the provisions that army contractors were to have placed along the route. In general, Ross believed it was better to be self-reliant than to depend on the army for provisions.

The committee negotiated with the government a contract that set a cost of $65.88 per person for the journey. This included the costs for wagons, horses, drivers, doctors, and other personnel. The committee explained that "the per capita expense of removal [was] based

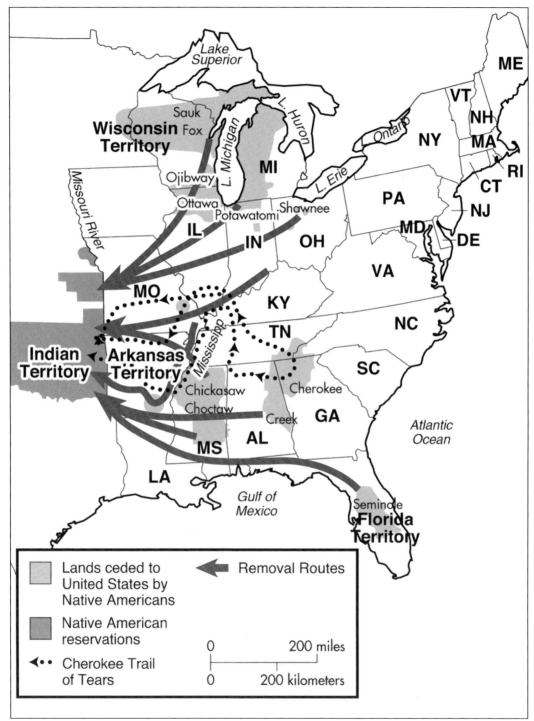

Lake Superior

ME

VT

NH

Sauk

Wisconsin Fox
Territory

L. Huron

L. Michigan

Ontario

NY

MA

RI

MI

L. Erie

PA

CT

NJ

Ojibway

Ottawa

Shawnee

MD

DE

Potawatomi

Missouri River

IL

IN

OH

VA

MO

KY

NC

TN

Mississippi

Indian
Territory

Arkansas
Territory

SC

Chickasaw

Cherokee

Choctaw

Creek

GA

Atlantic
Ocean

MS

AL

LA

Gulf of
Mexico

Seminole

Florida
Territory

	Lands ceded to United States by Native Americans		Removal Routes

Lands ceded to
United States by
Native Americans

Removal Routes

Native American
reservations

◄•• Cherokee Trail
of Tears

0   200 miles

0   200 kilometers

A map showing the lands given up by Native Americans as well as their removal routes on the way to the new Indian Territory.

Detachment of Cherokees During the 1838 Removal*

Detachment	Date of Departure	Count on Departure	Date of Arrival	Count on Arrival
Hair Conrad	August 28, 1838	729	January 17, 1839	654
Elijah Hicks	September 1	858	January 4	744
Jesse Bushyhead	September 3	950	February 27	898
John Benge	September 28	1,200	January 17	1,132
Situwakee	September 7	1,250	February 2	1,033
Old Field	September 24	983	February 23	921
Moses Daniel	September 20	1,035	March 2	924
Coowalooka	September 14	1,150	March ?	970
James Brown	September 10	850	March 5	717
George Hicks	September 7	1,118	March 14	1,039
Richard Taylor	September 20	1,029	March 24	942
Peter Hildebrand	October 23	1,766	March 24	1,311
John Drew	December 5	231	March 18	219

*Note: These were the official numbers. Other accounts had different numbers.

Taken from: William L. Anderson, ed., *Cherokee Removal: Before and After.* Athens: University of Georgia Press, 1991, p. 81.

on the calculation of one wagon & team & six riding horses being required for fifteen persons."[43]

The contract required the Cherokees to commence their travels by September 1 and be completed within two months. Scott gave a reprieve for those who were ill, however: "Such Indians as, within that time, may not be able to travel by land, shall . . . be permitted to remain until the next rise of waters."[44]

The Cherokees Leave the East

The attitude of the Cherokee people improved under their own leadership, but they knew that it would still be a long, hard journey ahead. The first of the thirteen detachments organized by John Ross set out on August 28, 1838, three days ahead of schedule. The second began a few days later, on September 1, and the third just two days after that. Other groups followed over the next couple of months; the last group did not depart until December. Each detachment was led by a Cherokee leader and was accompanied by a doctor. The missionaries who had lived among the Cherokees also went with some of the groups. U.S. soldiers rode alongside the procession and at the rear to make sure the group kept moving and did not turn back.

There were discrepancies between the official count of the army and that of Ross. For instance, the army officer counted 710, 859, and 846 people in the first, second, and third detachments; Ross counted 729, 858, and 950. Although the groups could decide their own route, all were substantially the same. Later groups often caught up to the group before them, and sometimes there was intermingling of the groups. Some Cherokees would join another group when they found friends or relatives. Others might stay behind to rest a few days and take up the march after a much-needed respite. The men would sometimes leave their group to hunt for deer, turkeys, or other food to supplement the

Under the guidance of Cherokee chief John Ross, thirteen detachments of Cherokees were scheduled to depart for the Indian Territory between September and December 1838.

army's meager rations. As a result, from the beginning, it was impossible to give an accurate count of how many people made the journey and how many died along the way.

A few wealthy Cherokees rode horses, and wagons carried those who were ill or too young to walk. But the vast majority of the emigrants walked. Day after day, rain or shine, the Cherokees trudged along the rustic roads.

Life on the Trail

An official trail to the new Cherokee land did not exist: Each detachment found its own way. Most groups traveled north and west across Tennessee and Kentucky, across southern Illinois and Missouri, and then into northeastern Indian Territory. This trip required the Cherokees to navigate difficult terrain. They would walk over mountains and hills and through vast tracts of wilderness. They also had to ford several rivers, including the mighty Mississippi.

The Cherokee groups were under orders to move quickly, but they could rarely travel more than 10 miles (16km) a day. Sometimes sickness forced groups to stop for several nights at a time. They also had to stop to bury the dead, often in shallow graves marked only by the tears of children or parents.

Even during the best conditions, the journey was tough. Camping required

Cherokees and other Native Americans suffered both physically and mentally on the difficult journey to the new land.

hard work. Cold and tired from walking all day, the Cherokees had to set up camp each evening. The following description from a missionary who accompanied the Cherokees gives a glimpse into what it was like to break camp:

> In the morning taking our own bed, etc. from the little wagon in which we sleep to the large wagon which carries it—replacing the seat—getting water—cooking breakfast, putting up things, harnessing, etc. Soon we are hurried on by the wagons we accompany to the next encampment. Here we have to undo what we did in the morning—put up our tent, get wood and water, prepare supper, fix our bed, etc.[45]

Cooking was difficult. Many families lacked pots, pans, or cooking utensils. Others did not know how to cook with flour, which was a main component of the government provisions. Sometimes there was too little food; other times, the food was well past its prime. Rebecca Neugin, who was just three when she made the journey with her family, later recalled:

> The people got so tired of eating salt pork on the journey that my father would walk through the woods as we traveled, hunting for turkeys and deer which he brought into camp to feed us. Camp was usually made at some place where water was to be had and when we stopped and prepared to cook our food, other emigrants who had been driven from their homes without opportunity to secure cooking utensils came to our camp to use our pots and kettles.[46]

Whereas the heat of summer had plagued the first expeditions, travel in fall and winter created its own problems. From October through early December, the expeditions set out for their new homes. The trip was supposed to take eighty days, but some of the groups took twice that long. Heavy rains hampered the groups and made travel difficult along the rutted, rustic roads. Wagons become stuck in the mud. A white traveler from Maine who happened upon one of the Cherokee groups in Kentucky wrote of the scene:

> We found the road literally filled with the procession for about three miles in length. The sick and feeble were carried in wagons . . . a great many ride horseback and multitudes go on foot—even aged females, apparently nearly ready to drop into the grave, were traveling with heavy burdens attached to the back—on the sometimes frozen ground, and sometimes muddy streets, with no covering for the feet except what nature had given them.[47]

As the contingents pushed westward, horses and other animals were lost. Wagon wheels broke. Sometimes wagons had to be abandoned, and people and possessions had to be moved to those that re-

General Winfield Scott

General Winfield Scott was put in charge of the removal of the Cherokees. He expected his troops to treat the Cherokee people fairly and kindly. His goal for the operation to go smoothly was undermined by vicious soldiers, unscrupulous traders, and harsh weather. Yet Scott's writings suggest that he believed the removal to have gone as well as it could have. In this excerpt from a memoir, Scott gives his view of the Cherokee people:

The Cherokees were an interesting people—the greater number Christians, and many as civilized as their neighbors of the white race. Between the two colors intermarriages had been frequent. They occupied a contiguous territory—healthy mountains, valleys, and plains lying in North Carolina, Georgia, Alabama, and Tennessee. Most of their leading men had received good educations and possessed much ability. Some were quite wealthy in cultivated farms, good houses, cattle seen everywhere, and the women graceful, with, in many cases, added beauty.

Quoted in Vicki Rozema, *Voices from the Trail of Tears.* New York: John F. Blair, 2003, p. 180.

mained. The wagons became more and more crowded. As people became ill, older Cherokees and women with small children gave up their places in the wagons to those with greater need. As the wagons jostled over the deeply rutted roads, those who were ill suffered greatly.

The travelers were at the mercy of the weather. There was no way to escape the rain, and the heat of the sun was not any better. For those who were sick, the harsh conditions made recovery almost impossible.

A Cold Winter

Most of the Cherokees had lived in the southeast their entire lives. They were unprepared for the cold they encountered on the northern route. The army was supposed to provide blankets, but there were not enough to go around. Missionary Evan Jones wrote in December, "It has … been exceedingly cold for some time past, which renders the condition of those who are but thinly clad, very uncomfortable."[48] To address this problem, the contingents often sent a small group of men ahead of the wagons to build fires at intervals along the road where the Cherokees could rest and warm themselves.

As winter set in, rivers froze over, making crossing hazardous. Some detachments had to camp by river's edge for days or weeks until the weather warmed up enough to make crossing the river possible. Several groups were stuck for a month in southern Illinois because

Winter presented many challenges to the Native Americans on the trail. Walking through the snow and ice was treacherous, food was scarce, and many died from exposure to the cold.

large chunks of ice on the Mississippi River made crossing impossible.

Food became scarce. Thousands of people lacked warm blankets, warm clothes, or shoes. As people huddled together in makeshift shelters, illness spread rapidly. Plagued by pneumonia and influenza, death became a daily companion. One expedition reported that fifteen to twenty people a night died of exposure. George Hicks, the leader of an expedition waiting for the ice to melt on the Mississippi, wrote in January, "We must necessarily calculate on suffering a great deal from hardships & exposure before we yet reach our homes in the far West . . . as we are hardly half way."[49]

Help and Hindrances Along the Way

Some of the white people whom the Cherokees passed helped them along the way. Alerted by the missionaries who had lived among the Cherokees, some church groups collected food and blankets and brought them to where the Cherokees camped. Some whites opened their homes and churches to shelter the weary travelers. One family took in a Cherokee woman and her friends when she went into labor and provided a home for her and her baby boy for a few weeks after the birth.

But not everyone was hospitable. Many whites were frightened of Indians and did not want them passing through their towns. The author of an 1838 article in the *Arkansas Gazette* wrote:

[The U.S. government] is sending thousands on thousands of Indians to be our immediate neighbor, and the greater portion of them have been driven from their homes east of the Mississippi, at the point of the

The Legend of the Cherokee Rose

According to legend, the women on the Trail of Tears grieved so much that they were unable to help their children. The Cherokee chiefs prayed for a sign that would lift the mothers' spirits and give them strength to care for their children. The next day, the travelers saw a beautiful rose where a mother's tear fell to the ground. From then on, a flower—a Cherokee rose—grew wherever a mother's tear landed. The Cherokee rose is white because this is the closest color to tears. The gold center represents the gold that was taken from Cherokee lands. Each stem of the Cherokee rose has seven leaves—one for each of the Cherokee clans.

The Cherokee rose continues to grow in the wild along the Trail of Tears. In 1968 the state of Georgia adopted the Cherokee rose as its official state floral emblem.

bayonet, and come here with the most embittered feelings toward the white people generally. Indeed, the great portion of them carry the marks of determined vengeance in their countenances, and no one can doubt that they will embrace the first opportunity that offers to wreak that vengeance on our unoffending citizens.[50]

Many whites took advantage of the Cherokees' situation, however. Stores charged unreasonably high prices for food and other supplies. The Cherokees were sometimes forced to pay twice the toll of a white for a ferry. A continuous stream of people waited to cross the rivers. Sometimes the ferry operators forced the Cherokees to wait until they had taken whites across. A broken wagon wheel forced the Cherokees to choose between paying an outrageous fee for a new wheel or leaving the wagon and its precious cargo behind. Some landowners demanded payment for crossing their land. Sometimes local residents demanded that the Cherokees pay them for property damage that had not occurred. George Hicks wrote from Tennessee, "Since we have been on our march many of us have been stopped and our horses taken from our Teams for the payment of unjust and past demands. Yet the government says you must go, and its citizens say you must pay me. Our property has been stolen and robbed by white men and no means given us to pay our debts."[51]

Hunger was a constant threat. The army had promised the Cherokees that food and other provisions would be placed at key points along the way, but the plan quickly went awry. When provisions were left too early along the trail, the Cherokees had to empty the wagons of their possessions to make room for it. The food was sometimes left for days or even weeks, and the Cherokees would arrive to find rotting meat and wormy corn. Moldy hay made the horses and other animals sick. Men and women became ill from drinking contaminated water. Some unscrupulous contractors simply ignored their order to provide food. As winter set in, it became impossible to hunt to supplement the provisions the army provided.

Liquor caused additional problems. Merchants followed the bands of Cherokees, selling them whiskey and moonshine. The agents accompanying the Cherokees often complained that men were too drunk to continue their travels. "The only source of annoyance upon the journey has resulted from the people obtaining liquor, the use of which with Indians as far as I have observed invariably results in rioting, fighting or disorder of some kind," complained Edward Deas, a lieutenant in charge of one of the early groups of emigrants. "As far as I have observed there is never any difficulty in managing Indians, when sober, provided they are properly treated; but when under the effects of liquor (in the use of which they have no moderation) they are unmanageable."[52]

Escape

Not all of the Cherokees obeyed orders to continue the westward trek. The army was plagued with desertions. This is part

Stand Watie

Stand Watie was born in 1806 in present-day Georgia. He believed that the Cherokees' best chance at survival was to cede their land in the southeast. Watie helped negotiate the 1835 Treaty of New Echota. He was among about two thousand Cherokees who moved voluntarily to Indian Territory in 1836. After the Trail of Tears, Watie was warned that a faction from the eastern Cherokees planned to kill the leaders of the Treaty Party for their role, and he fled to Arkansas. He was the only member of the Treaty Party to survive the attempted assassination and returned to lead a faction of Cherokees who opposed John Ross and his leadership.

Watie distinguished himself during the Civil War. He organized and led a cavalry of Cherokees known as the First Cherokee Mounted Rifles. These Cherokees fought diligently, not only against the Union forces but also against the Cherokees who had joined the Union army. He became one of only two Native Americans to achieve the rank of brigadier general in the Civil War. (The other was Ely S. Parker, a Seneca who fought on the side of the Union.) On June 23, 1865, Watie became the last Confederate general to surrender to Union troops.

Stand Watie.

of the reason why no one knows exactly how many Cherokees died along the way. Some of the people who did not arrive in Indian Territory with their groups had simply left the trail and escaped into the nearby wilderness. Seeing the long, dangerous road ahead, the escapees often tried to return the way they had come. Some took only what they could carry, but sometimes several dozen people would try to escape with wagonsful of food and supplies.

The Cherokee leaders of the groups often did little to dissuade people who wanted to leave the trail. They left this task to the U.S. troops. Some of the

The last group of Cherokees arrived in Indian Territory in March 1839, but no one knows how many died along the way from sickness, starvation, and hardships of the journey itself.

escapees were caught and continued the march under guard; others managed to escape into the woods.

One escapee was a North Carolina Cherokee named Junaluska (Tsunu'lahun'ski). He was among the 910 Cherokees who left under the leadership of a Cherokee Baptist minister named Jesse Bushyhead. Junaluska had served under the command of Andrew Jackson in the Creek War. He led about one hundred Cherokees who helped Jackson win the Battle of Horseshoe Bend in Alabama by swimming across a river and surprising the Creeks from behind. He was also credited with saving Jackson's life. Following the battle, Jackson reportedly told Junaluska, "As long as the sun shines and the grass grows, there shall be friendship between us, and the feet of the Cherokee shall be toward the east."[53]

On October 26, 1838, Junaluska and about fifty others informed Bushyhead that they intended to return to North Carolina. Bushyhead did not use force to stop them as they left the trail with fifty wagons because, said the official report, "he did not think it his duty to do so."[54]

Junaluska and twenty-five of his comrades were captured near Knoxville and taken as prisoners to Fort Cass. Junaluska was put in irons and sent west under guard of the soldiers who were to be stationed at Fort Gibson in Indian Territory. Still, Junaluska returned east. He reportedly said, "If I had known that Jackson would drive us from our homes, I would have killed him that day at the Horseshoe."[55]

Junaluska's service paid off, however. In 1847 he was granted North Carolina citizenship and given a tract of land in the mountains. The many other Cherokees who settled in North Carolina were not as lucky, however. They had to wait many years to be recognized as citizens of the state.

A New Home at Last

On March 24, 1839, the last group of Cherokees arrived in the west. They had spent more than five months on the road. No one knows exactly how many deaths occurred during the journey. Elizur Butler, a doctor who accompanied one of the detachments, estimated that nearly one-fifth of the Cherokee population died. The trip was particularly hard on the elderly, children, and infants. The travelers died from colds, influenza, measles, fevers, dysentery, whooping cough, and cholera. Others died in accidents, from starvation, and due to other hardships of the journey. Many of those who died on the passage were hastily buried in unmarked graves; others had to be left unburied along the road.

Many of those who died were too poor to afford the bare necessities, but no one was immune from the suffering. John Ross lost his beloved wife, Quatie, for instance, who had given her blanket to a young child. Quatie had been ill before traveling, and the hardships of the trip proved too much for her. One writer said that Quatie Ross was among the many Cherokee women "who had been as gently reared as any white woman and was no more fit for winter travel by wagon and horseback than anyone else not used to hardship."[56]

Chapter Five

Starting Over

When the Cherokee people finally reached Indian Territory, they no doubt felt great relief to have the long, hard days of walking behind them. After months of difficult and harrowing travel, they could finally focus on the future and begin to carve out a new life for themselves. There remained many challenges, however. The land in Indian Territory was not as fertile as the land they had left behind. The government had promised to supply the Cherokees with food for a year after their arrival—until they had time to plant and harvest their first crops. Private contractors were hired to ration the supplies, however, and unscrupulous contractors stole much of what was to be given to the Native Americans. Contractors also cut corners by buying cheap food and sometimes failed to store it properly, resulting in provisions that included rotting meat and moldy corn and flour.

Sickness continued to plague the Cherokees. Nearby tribes were suffering from smallpox and other diseases, and hundreds of Cherokees—weakened from their exhausting trip—succumbed to illness. Many died soon after their arrival. They did not have doctors, and many of the herbs and remedies that medicine men had used in the southeastern United States could not be found in Oklahoma. Many more died of malnutrition and starvation because of corrupt agents who were supposed to supply them with necessities.

The task before the Cherokee people was daunting. Like the Native Americans who had come before them, the survivors of the Trail of Tears had to rebuild their homes and farms, roads and bridges, and shops and businesses on the new, foreign land they had been granted. They had to forge a new government and justice system, build new schools, and establish a new community.

The Old Settlers

When the groups of Cherokees arrived in Indian Territory in 1839, they joined thousands of Cherokees who came before them. Since 1794, small groups of Cherokees had moved westward. At first they settled in present-day Arkansas, but an 1828 treaty with the U.S. government forced them farther west to the northwestern corner of present-day Oklahoma. U.S. government officials hoped that these early settlers could encourage the Cherokees who remained in the east to join them. Over the next several years, small groups of Cherokees voluntarily left their homes to join the western Cherokees.

Earlier, in 1819, the Cherokees in the east had formally disowned these Cherokees and refused to recognize them as part of the Cherokee Nation. The western Cherokees—who became known as the Old Settlers—elected their own chiefs and passed their own laws. Naturally, the Old Settlers wanted to continue following their own leaders and laws.

Still, with the arrival of the Cherokees in 1839, the Old Settlers were vastly outnumbered. The new arrivals had no intention of subjecting themselves to the rule of the minority who were already established in Indian Territory. "Those in the West in 1838 constituted only one-third of the tribe," writes historian

Remembering One's Heritage

Unlike most other Native American groups, the Cherokees encouraged members to marry white settlers. Many of the Cherokees alive today are descended from early white settlers. In the following excerpt from a 1970 interview published in the St. Louis Post-Dispatch, *Jack Bushyhead, the grandson of a famous Cherokee chief, tells what it is like to be Cherokee:*

My grandmother the Chief's wife, used to want me to sit at her knees for hours while she tried to tell me stories about our people. I wish that I had listened, but at that time it didn't seem important. But as I grow older I am more interested in preserving our heritage, not particularly for myself, but out of respect for those who were my people. I don't think of myself in terms of being an Indian, but I'm conscious of things that pertain to them. For example, I've noticed in movies and on TV that when white men win a battle it's called a great victory; when Indians win one it's called a massacre. I think of myself as being strictly American, which I am, literally.

Quoted in Elizabeth Mulligan, "Accounts of the 'Cherokee Trail of Tears' with Reference to 'Princess Otahki,'" *St. Louis Post-Dispatch*, January 18, 1970. www.thepeoplespaths.net/articles/princes.html.

William G. McLoughlin. "It would hardly do for their chiefs and laws and council to remain in power once the 14,000 emigrants from the ancient homeland arrived."[57]

The eastern Cherokees wanted to continue to follow their own written constitution, laws, and elected leaders. Before leaving for their new western homes, they adopted a resolution declaring "that the inherent sovereignty of the Cherokee Nation [that is, the easterners], together with its constitution, laws and usages of the same are in full force and virtue and shall continue in perpetuity [forever]."[58]

The Struggle for Unity

In April 1839 Chief John Ross proposed that a joint council be held to carve out a new, unified government. On June 3, 1839, more than six thousand Cherokees met to discuss what should be done. John Brown, one of the chiefs of the Old Settlers, publicly welcomed the new arrivals:

> We joyfully welcome you to our country. The whole land is before you. You may go freely wherever you choose and select any places for settlement which you may please. . . . Next July will be an election . . . for members of both houses of our legislature. At those elections you will be voters. . . . [Meanwhile] it is expected that you will be subject to our government and laws." [59]

Although the eastern Cherokees were to be given the right to vote in the next elections, Ross was opposed to the suggestion that the eastern Cherokees would no longer be governed by the laws they had already written.

Thus began a difficult negotiation process between the chiefs of the two factions. Ross rejected Brown's subsequent proposal that the two bands continue to be governed separately because he believed this would weaken their position with the U.S. government and create confusion and conflict among the Cherokees. As an alternative, he proposed having a committee write a new code of law for the unified Cherokee Nation. He suggested having a committee of nine create the new laws: Three representatives would be elected by the western Cherokees, three by the eastern faction, and the remaining three would be selected by these six. The new laws would then be presented to the Cherokee people for approval. Brown worried that this would give the eastern Cherokees a clear advantage because they were in the majority.

One of the reasons it was important to decide who was in charge was because the U.S. government owed the Cherokees money. The government had promised to pay the Cherokees for their land and to support them during their initial months in Indian Territory. Each of the two factions believed that they should be in charge of the funds. The leaders of the Old Settlers wrote a letter to Montfort Stokes, the U.S. agent in charge of the funds, requesting that he pay them the funds. The eastern Cherokees were outraged. The leaders of the eastern faction wrote their own letter to

Stokes, asking that he not disburse any money "until a reunion of the people shall be effected."[60]

The anger on the part of the easterners was fueled by the fact that the Old Settlers counted among their numbers the leaders who had signed the Treaty of New Echota. The eastern Cherokees believed that this treaty had robbed them of their land. They viewed the men who had negotiated the treaty as traitors and blamed them for the many hardships the Cherokee people had endured over the past several months.

The members of the Treaty Party knew they were in danger. John Schermerhorn, the negotiator of the Treaty of New Echota, later recalled what John Ridge had said to him during a visit in early 1839:

> You for what you have done, have been abused, misrepresented and slandered by your countrymen, and I might yet someday die by the hand of some poor infatuated Indian, deluded by the counsels of Ross . . . but we have this to console us, we shall have suffered and died in a good cause. My people are now free and happy in their new homes, and I am resigned to my fate, whatever it might be.[61]

The Treaty Signers Are Sentenced to Death

On June 21 a group of about one hundred Cherokees met secretly to discuss the situation. They wanted to punish the signers of the Treaty of New Echota. Some argued that they should enforce the Cherokee law that called for the death of anyone selling tribal land. The group drew up a list of the leaders who they believed to be responsible for the Treaty of New Echota. A trial was held for Elias Boudinot, Major Ridge, John Ridge, Stand Watie, James Starr, John Adair Bell, and George W. Adair, without any of them knowing anything about it. All of the defendants were condemned to death. A committee planned the executions. Lots were drawn to decide who would execute each man.

At dawn the next day, the groups of assassins set out. One group of men went to John Ridge's house, where they brutally stabbed him to death. The group looking for Elias Boudinot asked him for medicine. As he went to the storehouse to get the medicine, the assassins ambushed him, killing him with their knives and tomahawks. A friend of Boudinot saw the attack and sent someone to warn Boudinot's brother, Stand Watie, that he might be next. Watie was the only one sentenced to death who escaped. A group of ten or twelve assassins shot Major Ridge on his return from visiting one of his slaves who was sick in nearby Arkansas.

Although the leaders of the Treaty Party were caught unawares, they were not entirely unprepared for their fate. John Schermerhorn, a minister who was instrumental in negotiating the treaty on behalf of the U.S. government, later wrote, "These men, before they entered upon their business, knew they were

A group of Cherokees, angry about the brutal journey to the new land, decided to kill the signers of the Treaty of New Echota, blaming those signers for the forced migration. John Ridge, pictured, was among the group of signers who was murdered.

running a dreadful risk, for it was death by their laws for any person to enter into a treaty with the United States." After Major Ridge signed the document, he said to his colleagues, "I have just signed my death warrant."[62]

Retaliation

The killings had a number of repercussions. Historian William G. McLoughlin writes, "Their deaths caused an immediate panic among all members of the Treaty party, a vehement reaction by the federal government [which had promised to protect the treaty supporters], and general horror among the white American public."[63] Word of the attacks spread quickly through the community. Many supporters of the Treaty Party fled to Arkansas. Others took up arms and vowed revenge.

Friends and relatives of the victims blamed John Ross for the murders. They believed that Ross had ordered the killings. Watie had gathered a group to retaliate by killing Ross. Ross insisted that he did not know who the executioners were and expressed regret for the

A Message from the Chief

The Cherokee people have not forgotten the Trail of Tears. During ceremonies and celebrations, they take time from their busy lives to remember the event and what it meant for their people. In 2009 a group of eight Cherokee students rode bicycles along the Trail of Tears from Tennessee to Oklahoma. Principal Chief Chadwick "Corntassel" Smith discusses the importance of the event:

When our ancestors made the trek from Georgia to Indian Territory back in the winter of 1838–39, they had no choice. The conditions of their travel included extreme weather, unscrupulous merchants along the way who took advantage by inflating their prices, camp owners who refused to let our people cut wood for fires in the dead of winter, grueling climbs, attacks from wild animals, chronic sickness and, all too often, death. Yet, in spite of all, our Cherokee people managed to not only complete their thousand-mile [1,609km] exodus from their homelands, they faced all types of adversity, survived, adapted, prospered and excelled in their new territory. Our people rose up and found strength within themselves to become business and industry leaders, build schools, create an unparalleled free education system, forge a court and legal system and in general, became a model society.

Chad Smith, "Message from Principal Chief Chad Smith," Remember the Removal Project. www.remembertheremoval.org/Remember/Chief_Message.html.

murders. He wrote to General Matthew Arbuckle at Fort Gibson for protection. This was not needed, however, because almost immediately a group of about two hundred of Ross's supporters converged at his home to defend him from any attempts on his life.

The Treaty Party believed the armed men at Ross's home were planning more murders. Now they appealed to Arbuckle for help. Federal troops were sent to Cherokee territory to help keep the peace.

On July 1, a meeting was held. Many members of the Treaty Party, including Stand Watie, were afraid to attend. Ross wanted to use this meeting to call a truce. He knew that the survival of the Cherokee Nation depended on peace between the warring factions. At the meeting, the council called for amnesty for the murderers of the Ridges and Boudinot. The council then asked the signers of the Treaty of New Echota to come forward and apologize for signing the treaty. Eight men came forward, but the rest of the Treaty Party refused. Stand Watie was among those who contended that they had acted in the best interests of the Cherokee Nation.

Unity at Last

Against the growing odds of success, Ross continued to work for unity of the Cherokee factions. A number of meetings were held to persuade Cherokees on both sides to vote for unity. Finally, on July 12, the Act of Union was adopted. The act stated, "We the people, composing the Eastern and Western Cherokee Nation[s], in National Convention assembled, by

In September 1839 both sides of the Cherokee Nation—those against the migration treaty and those in favor of it— united under one government.

virtue of our original and inalienable rights, do hereby solemnly and mutually agree to form ourselves into one body politic under the style and title of the Cherokee Nation."[64]

On September 19 the newly elected council of the reunited Cherokee Nation held its first meeting in the new capital of Tahlequah and took power as the official government.

Protests Continue

Many Cherokees contested the sovereignty of the new government. For many years, the Old Settlers refused to follow its laws. They believed that the legitimate government was the one that was in place before the new 1838 emigration.

Members of the Treaty Party also were against a united government, mostly because they did not favor John Ross as its leader. Under the leadership of Stand Watie, this faction continued to fight against Ross's followers. Conflict between the two factions often led to bloodshed. Although the new government warned against revenge killings, many Cherokees responded to violence with violence. In one nine-month period, thirty-three murders were reported. The warring factions pointed fingers at one another for the violence.

The Cherokees might have continued fighting for many more years had they not realized that it was putting their very survival at risk. Conflict within the Cherokee community made it difficult to defend the nation against external threats. The Cherokees worried that one faction would again side with the U.S. government or white communities against the other side. Both sides realized that there was strength in numbers. In 1846 the two sides—represented by long-time adversaries Ross and Watie—signed a treaty recognizing the Cherokee Nation as one group.

The Task at Hand

Governance was just one problem among many for the Cherokees in Indian Territory. Families set about building log cabins and clearing the land for farms. Hunting, which the Cherokees had given up as part of the assimilation program in the East, once again became an important skill. Few Cherokees had shoes; once again they relied on animal hide to make moccasins and breeches. Because the Cherokees had been forced to turn over their guns and rifles to army personnel, they used the bows and arrows, traps, and other weapons of their forefathers to catch game.

The Cherokees had been able to bring little with them over the Trail of Tears, and so they had to reconstruct almost everything from scratch. "Very few of the Indians had been able to bring any of their household effects or kitchen utensils with them," one Cherokee later recalled. "So the old people, who knew how, made what they called 'dirt pots' and 'dirt bowls.' . . . [Then] they made wooden spoons, and for a number of years after we arrived we had to use these crude utensils."[65]

A New Society

Despite these inauspicious beginnings, the Cherokee people survived—even thrived. In Indian Territory, the Cherokees soon rebuilt a democratic form of government, churches, schools, newspapers, and businesses. During what some historians call the Cherokee Golden Age, Tahlequah, the new Cherokee capital, and nearby Park Hill became business and cultural centers of activity.

The Cherokees brought with them their experience in the east and built an educated, enlightened society in the wilderness into which they were thrown. The homes they built in their new land were like the homes of white men. They built churches, divided the new country into voting districts, and wrote a new constitution. In 1844 the *Cherokee Advocate*, printed in both the Cherokee and English languages, became the first

Despite the tremendous difficulties endured by the Cherokee people during their forced journey to Indian Territory, they slowly rebuilt their society and were able to thrive.

newspaper in Indian Territory. By the time of the Civil War, there were twenty-one elementary and secondary schools for Cherokees. The educational system rivaled those of white communities. In fact, many white settlements bordering the Cherokee Nation took advantage of the superior school system and paid tuition to have their children attend the Cherokee schools.

The Civil War

The relative peace and prosperity of the Cherokee Nation would not last long. In 1861 the Civil War broke out between the North and the South. Chief John Ross asked the United States to send troops to protect its neutrality as promised in the treaty, but this was yet another promise the United States failed to keep. The leaders of the Treaty Party sided with the Confederacy and convinced Ross to sign a formal alliance with the South. Other Cherokees fought on the side of the Union, pitting one faction of Cherokees against another. The Cherokees were heavily involved in the fighting that took place in and near In-dian Territory. Historians estimate that the Cherokee Nation lost as much as one-third of its population during the Civil War.

The Cherokee people lost more than lives as a result of the war. When the North emerged as victors, the Cherokee Nation was treated as a defeated enemy. The United States used the Cherokees' alliance with the South to punish the Cherokees, taking more than half of the land that had been promised them. Certain governmental powers also were taken away from the Cherokee Nation.

Westward Expansion

As the United States continued to grow, Cherokee land continued to be threatened. Once again old treaties were broken, and new treaties were forced upon

This late nineteeth-century political cartoon shows how westward expansion by white settlers, railroad companies, and the U.S. government was injust to Native Americans.

Cherokee leaders. The U.S. government used its power of eminent domain to take land from the Cherokee Nation to make way for railroads needed to move people and goods to the new areas opening in the west.

The Indian Territory had been intended as a place where Indians could live separately from whites. But whites soon moved to the uninhabited part of the territory, claiming the land for themselves. By 1880 more whites than Indians lived in Indian Territory.

In the late 1800s, what remained of Cherokee tribal land was divided into individual allotments and given to the Cherokees who were listed in the official census. Unscrupulous white speculators swindled many of these Cherokees out of their newly acquired land. The Cherokee people today live on less than one-third of 1 percent of the 7 million acres (2.83 million ha) granted to them by the Treaty of New Echota.

The Cherokee Nation was officially dissolved in 1906, and Indian Territory was combined with Oklahoma Territory to form the new state of Oklahoma. Against their wishes, the Cherokees became citizens of Oklahoma and the United States.

Still, the people fiercely clung to their identity as Cherokees and craved their independence. In 1948 a new Cherokee Nation emerged. Since that time, the Cherokee people have struggled to obtain self-governance. They remind Americans that they are a civilized people and are more than capable of governing themselves. After all, they existed as an independent nation long before the United States came into being.

The Cherokee Nation Today

Three distinct, federally recognized tribes exist today: the Cherokee Nation, the United Keetoowah Band, and the East-

ern Band. With more than three hundred thousand tribal members, the Cherokee Nation is the largest Native American tribe in the United States and Canada. Most members of the Cherokee Nation live in northeastern Oklahoma, in 7,000 square miles (18,130 sq. km) that were part of the area granted by the Treaty of New Echota. Another twenty thousand Cherokees make up the Eastern Band of

Cherokees today take pride in their heritage. Shown here, Cherokee dancers perform in their native dress at the Chehaw National Indian Festival in Albany, Georgia.

Cherokee Indians and live on a Cherokee reservation in North Carolina. Most of these Cherokees are descended from those who avoided the Trail of Tears by escaping into the mountains or agreeing to exchange Cherokee citizenship for U.S. citizenship.

The Cherokees have been in contact with people of European descent for more than four hundred years. More than perhaps any other Native American group, the Cherokees married white settlers and adopted white customs. Today, many Cherokees blend with their white neighbors as they commute from their land in Oklahoma and North Carolina to jobs in nearby cities. Others have left the land they were given in Oklahoma and have settled across America and around the world. In cities, suburbs, and rural areas, the Cherokees work and play alongside whites, often indistinguishable as a minority culture.

Despite their past hardships, the Cherokees have thrived as a people. They have become business and industry leaders. The Cherokee Nation established the first free, compulsory public school system and built the first university west of the Mississippi River. The Cherokee Nation's government, based on a new constitution ratified in 1975, governs equitably and judiciously.

Even while adopting white customs, however, the Cherokees have clung to their heritage. They take pride in their culture and honor their history. In Cherokee, North Carolina, the Eastern Band of Cherokees hosts an annual Cherokee Indian Fair to showcase the Cherokees' re-markable culture and heritage. Traditional Cherokees also gather periodically at consecrated ceremonial grounds, called stomp grounds, where they take part in a series of dances around the sacred fire. Some Cherokees perform the stomp dances publicly as part of their effort to teach people about traditional Cherokee ways and beliefs. The Red Clay Council Ground, the site of the last Cherokee council meetings before removal, was acquired by the state of Tennessee and is now a state park. The park includes a museum and outdoor replicas of a Cherokee council house from the 1830s, sleeping huts, and a farmstead.

Remembering the Trail of Tears

The removal of the Cherokee people is a crucial part of Cherokee history and its collective memory. Historians say we must understand history in order not to repeat it. A sympathetic soldier who participated in the removal agrees. "Murder is murder and someone must answer," he wrote years later. "Somebody must explain the streams of blood that flowed in the Indian country in the summer of 1838. Somebody must explain the four-thousand silent graves that mark the trail of the Cherokees to their exile."[66]

Cherokees and Americans have revisited the Trail of Tears to learn about how it happened and how to prevent such horror in the future. As Wilma Mankiller, a former chief of the Cherokee Nation, writes, "Although it is so crucial for us to focus on the good things—our tenacity, our language and culture, the revital-

"TRAIL OF TEARS"

AFTER CONGRESS PASSED THE INDIAN REMOVAL ACT, MAY 28, 1830, THE GOVERNMENT FORCEABLY RELOCATED ABOUT 60,000 INDIANS FROM THE SOUTHEASTERN U.S. TO WHAT IS NOW OKLAHOMA. THIS INCLUDED THE FIVE (5) CIVILIZED TRIBES: CHEROKEE, CHICKASAW, CREEK, CHOCTAW AND SEMINOLE.

WHEN ANDREW JACKSON RAN FOR PRESIDENT IN 1828, HE PLEDGED TO MOVE THE INDIANS WEST OF THE MISSISSIPPI RIVER. AFTER REMOVAL BECAME LAW, THE GOVERNMENT PROCEEDED TO RELOCATE THE INDIANS.

SOME TRAVELLED OVERLAND AND OTHERS BY WATER. MANY SUFFERED SEVERE HARDSHIPS.

ABOUT 14,000 CHEROKEES WERE RELOCATED WITH 4,000 DEATHS OCCURING. THE GRIEF FROM THEIR LOVED ONES' DEATHS, THE HARDSHIPS AND DEPRIVATIONS, MADE THEIR TREK WESTWARD INDEED A "TRAIL OF TEARS".

ERECTED BY CONWAY CHAMBER OF COMMERCE
FAULKNER COUNTY HISTORICAL SOCIETY
IN COOPERATION WITH U.S. ARMY CORPS OF ENGINEERS
OCTOBER, 1989

This Trail of Tears memorial overlooks the Arkansas River in Conway, Arkansas.

ization of tribal communities—it is also important that we never forget what happened to our people on the Trail of Tears. It was indeed our holocaust."[67]

One hundred and seventy years after they were forced to march along dusty, muddy, and frozen roads, the Cherokee people remember the Trail of Tears and honor both those who survived and those who perished on the journey. Most families have stories of ancestors who made the difficult journey and continue to feel the sting of injustice when they remember the loss of their ancestral homeland. Stories of removal figure prominently not only in their history but in their songs, art, literature, and plays as well. The Trail of Tears Singing is a gospel music festival that takes place in western North Carolina, where the ancestors of the Eastern Band avoided removal.

The Cherokee Nation has taken great measures to preserve official documents, letters, and diaries of those on the Trail of Tears. The Cherokees also have conducted interviews of those who made the

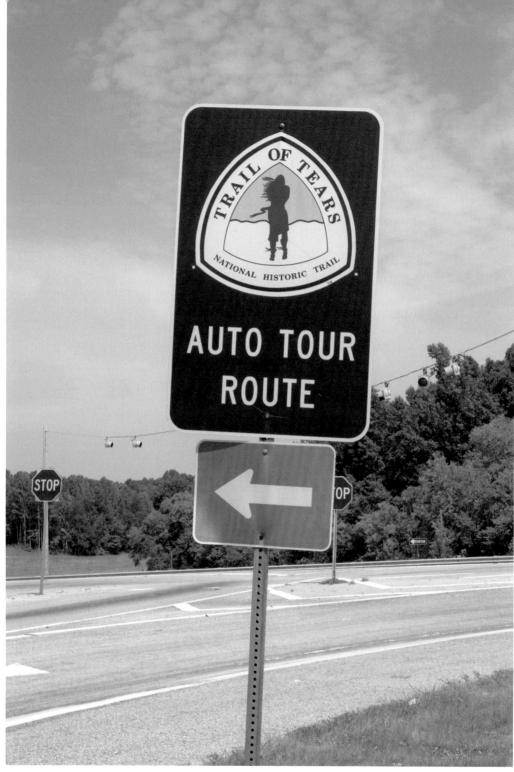

In 1987 Congress designated the Trail of Tears as a National Historic Trail.

journey to preserve their recollections in perpetuity. In 1963 the Cherokees established the Cherokee National Historical Society to preserve the history and culture of the Cherokee people. The society's work is done primarily through the Cherokee Heritage Center in Park Hill, Oklahoma. The center's Cherokee National Museum maintains a permanent Trail of Tears exhibit, replicas of ancient villages and farms, and temporary exhibits of Cherokee culture and art.

Many individuals have also sought to honor those who died along the trail. Early descendants returned to the Trail of Tears to mark the graves of their loved ones. Later descendants have visited points along the trail or followed it in commemoration of the Cherokees who suffered the journey. In 1984 a group of Cherokee students retraced the route of the Trail of Tears on bicycles. During the summer of 2009, eight young Cherokee cyclists re-created this "Remember the Removal" ride. The riders spent twenty-three days traveling from Tennessee to Oklahoma, averaging 40 to 70 miles (64 to 113km) a day. The riders stopped daily to learn about things that happened along the Trail of Tears. According to organizers, the purpose of the ride is to promote awareness of the Trail of Tears, to

Famous Cherokees in Recent History

M any Cherokees have assimilated into white culture. They can be found in all areas of life. Some have assumed great fame, although most people do not know they are Cherokees. Will Rogers, a Cherokee who was born in Indian Territory in 1879, was among the most famous Americans of his day. His excellent roping skills earned him renown as a performer in Wild West shows. He later starred in several movies. As a newspaper columnist and author of six books, Rogers is perhaps best remembered for his witticisms.

More recent Cherokee descendants who have achieved fame on the silver screen include Cher, James Garner, Dennis Weaver, and Kevin Costner, who earned acclaim for his starring role in *Dances with Wolves*. Country singing superstar Loretta Lynn and rock legend Jimi Hendrix, who was proud of his ancestry, also had Cherokee ancestors. Other claims to Cherokee descent are more tenuous. President Bill Clinton, teen idol Miley Cyrus, and actor Johnny Depp are among the many people who claim to have a Cherokee ancestor in the distant past. Given the number of intermarriages between Cherokees and whites (as well as blacks), there are probably many Americans who are unaware of their Cherokee ancestry.

educate Cherokee students about their tribe's tragic history, and to promote the achievements of the modern Cherokee Nation to those along the route.

Others have followed the trail on their own. In 1989, for example, Jerry Ellis, a Cherokee descendant, decided he would follow the path his ancestors took along the Trail of Tears. During the 1,000-mile (1,609km) journey, he slept in a tent in the woods, fished in streams, and foraged in the woods for food. Ellis wrote about his journey in a book called *Walking the Trail*.

Cherokees and whites commemorate the Trail of Tears in many other ways. Members of the Cherokee Nation often take time out to remember the ordeal and those who died along the way. Historical societies and state government agencies in Georgia, Tennessee, Alabama, Arkansas, Missouri, and other states have researched the paths the Cherokees and other Native American groups took on their way west and have published their own accounts and histories. In 1987 Congress designated the Trail of Tears as a National Historic Trail, leading the National Park Service and local and regional organizations to locate and mark historic sites related to Indian removal and the graves of those who traveled the trail.

The state of Missouri set aside 3,415 acres (1,382ha) of land in Cape Girardeau County as the Trail of Tears State Park. Most of the detachments traveled through Cape Girardeau County as they made their way west. According to legend, Nancy Bushyhead Walker Hildebrand died and was buried within the park's boundaries. She was the sister of the Reverend Jesse Bushyhead, who led one of the detachments, and the wife of Lewis Hildebrand, who led another. Hildebrand's two children continued the journey. The Trail of Tears State Park includes the Bushyhead Memorial as a tribute to her and to all the other Cherokees who died on the trail.

None of these measures can compensate for the lives lost and the hearts broken along the Trail of Tears, however. Only those who made the journey can truly understand what they lost and the new lives they built at the end of the trail. As a new century unfolds, the Cherokee people continue their centuries-old struggle to prepare for what the future holds without turning their backs on the past. "It was a spirit of survival and perseverance that carried the Cherokee to Indian Territory on the Trail of Tears," proclaims the Cherokee Nation's Web site. "Today, it is the same spirit leading the Cherokee."[68]

Notes

Introduction: What Is the Trail of Tears?

1. Quoted in Margaret Locklair, "North Carolina's Native Heritage," Primidia Publications, p. 3. http://away. com/ primedia/pol_soc/cherokee_3.adp.
2. Quoted in William L. Anderson, ed., *Cherokee Removal: Before and After.* Athens: University of Georgia Press, 1991, p. 93.

Chapter One: The Cherokees at Home

3. Ken Martin, "First European Contact," History of the Cherokee, 1996. www.cherokeehistory.com/firstcon.h tml.
4. Jerry Ellis, *Walking the Trail: One Man's Journey Along the Cherokee Trail of Tears.* New York: Delacorte, 1991.
5. Theda Perdue and Michael D. Green, *The Cherokee Removal: A Brief History with Documents.* Boston: Bedford/St. Martin's, 2005, p. 4.
6. Perdue and Green, *The Cherokee Removal*, p. 3.
7. Readers' Digest Editors, *Through Indian Eyes: The Untold Story of Native American Peoples.* Pleasantville, NY: Reader's Digest, 1995, p. 137.
8. Quoted in Ken Martin, "1700 Through the Revolutionary War," History of the Cherokee, 1996. www.cherokee history.com/1700thro.html.
9. Martin, "1700 Through the Revolutionary War."
10. Quoted in Knox County, TN, Archives History, "Chapter IV: Founding of Nashville," *Standard History of Knoxville.* http://files.usgwar chives.org/tn/knox/history/1900/ standard/founding2nms.txt.
11. Quoted in Perdue and Green, *The Cherokee Removal*, p. 11.
12. Joan Gilbert, *The Trail of Tears Across Missouri.* Columbia: University of Missouri Press, 1996, p. 6.

Chapter Two: The Path Toward Removal

13. Quoted in Gilbert, *The Trail of Tears Across Missouri*, p. 10.
14. In Perdue and Green, *The Cherokee Removal*, p. 61.
15. Quoted in Carole Bucy, "Cherokee Constitution," History 2020—American History, Volunteer State Community College. www2.volstate.edu/ cbucy/History%202030/Documents /Cherokee%20Constitution- Doc52.htm.
16. Quoted in James D. Richardson, ed., *A Compilation of the Messages and Papers of the Presidents.* New York: Bureau of National Literature, 1897, p. 1020. http://lincoln.lib.niu.edu/all .html.
17. Quoted in Elizabeth Mulligan, "Accounts of the 'Cherokee Trail of Tears'

with Reference to 'Princess Otahki,'" *St. Louis Post-Dispatch*, January 18, 1970. www.thepeoplespaths.net/articles/princes.html.

18. Quoted in Perdue and Green, *The Cherokee Removal*, p. 127.
19. Quoted in Philip B. Kurland and Ralph Lerner, eds., "Article 1, Section 8, Clause 3 (Indians), Document 10: *Cherokee Nation v. Georgia*," *The Founders' Constitution*. http://press-pubs.uchicago.edu/founders/documents/a1_8_3_indianss10.html.
20. Quoted in Gilbert, *Trail of Tears Across Missouri*, p. 14.

Chapter Three: Moving Out

21. Quoted in Thurman Wilkins, *Cherokee Tragedy: The Ridge Family and the Decimation of a People*. Norman: University of Oklahoma Press, 1986, p. 287.
22. Quoted in Vicki Rozema, *Voices from the Trail of Tears*. New York: John F. Blair, 2003, p. 15.
23. Quoted in About North Georgia, "Major Ridge." http://ngeorgia.com/ang/Major_Ridge.
24. Charles J. Kappler, *Indian Affairs: Laws and Treaties*. Vol. 2, *Treaties*. Washington, DC: Government Printing Office, 1904. http://digital.library.okstate.edu/KAPPLER/VOL2/treaties/che0439.htm#mn2, page 440.
25. Kappler, *Indian Affairs*, p. 443.
26. Kappler, *Indian Affairs*, p. 439.
27. Quoted in Learn NC, "Chief John Ross Protests the Treaty of New Echota," University of North Carolina, Chapel Hill. www.learnnc.org/lp/editions/nchist-newnation/4500.
28. Quoted in Cherokee Nation, "Ralph Waldo Emerson's Letter." www.cherokee.org/Culture/126/Page/default.aspx.
29. Quoted in Rozema, *Voices from the Trail of Tears*, p. 17.
30. Quoted in Rozema, *Voices from the Trail of Tears*, p. 68.
31. Quoted in Gilbert, *The Trail of Tears Across Missouri*, p. 32.
32. Quoted in Perdue and Green, *The Cherokee Removal*, p. 164.
33. Quoted in Rozema, *Voices from the Trail of Tears*, p. 20.
34. Quoted in Rozema, *Voices from the Trail of Tears*, p. 180.
35. Quoted in Rozema, *Voices from the Trail of Tears*, pp. 180–81.
36. Quoted in Perdue and Green, *The Cherokee Removal*, p. 173.
37. Quoted in Cherokee by Blood, "Trail of Tears." www.cherokeebyblood.com/trailtears.htm.
38. Quoted in Perdue and Green, *The Cherokee Removal*, p. 172.
39. Quoted in Rozema, *Voices from the Trail of Tears*, p. 28.
40. Quoted in Rozema, *Voices from the Trail of Tears*, p. 27.

Chapter Four: The Long Journey

41. Quoted in Cherokee by Blood, "Trail of Tears."
42. Rozema, *Voices from The Trail of Tears*, p. 117.
43. Rozema, *Voices from The Trail of Tears*, p. 120.
44. Quoted in Rozema, *Voices from The Trail of Tears*, p. 122.
45. Quoted in Gilbert, *Trail of Tears Across Missouri*, pp. 49–50.
46. Quoted in Anderson, ed., *Cherokee Removal*, p. 81.
47. Quoted in John Ehle, *The Trail of Tears:*

The Rise and Fall of the Cherokee Nation. New York: Anchor, 1988, p. 358.

48. Quoted in American Native Press Archives, "Evan Jones to the American Baptist Missionary Board, Little Prairie, Missouri, December 30, 1838," University of Arkansas, Little Rock. http://anpa.ualr.edu/trailOf Tears/letters/1838December30Evan JonestoTheAmericanBaptistMission aryBoard.htm.

49. Quoted in Perdue and Green, *The Cherokee Removal,* p. 177.

50. Quoted in American Native Press Archives, "Dissatisfaction Among the Indians, *Arkansas Gazette,* May 30, 1838," University of Arkansas, Little Rock. http://anpa.ualr.edu/trail_ of_tears/indian_removal_project/pu blic_opinion/dissatisfaction.htm.

51. Quoted in "Letter by George Hicks Dated Nov. 4th, 1838, to John Ross," NAAIP Paths to Living History, The People's Paths Home Page, www .thepeoplespaths.net/history/hicks .html.

52. Edward Deas, "Journal of Occurrences: April–May 1838," American Native Press Archives, University of Arkansas, Little Rock. http://anpa .ualr.edu/trail_of_tears/indian_remo val_project/eye_witness_accounts/e ye-witness5.htm.

53. Quoted in Cherokee North Carolina, "Junaluska." www.cherokee-nc.com/ index.php?page=58.

54. Quoted in Rozema, *Voices from the Trail of Tears,* p. 171.

55. Quoted in Cherokee North Carolina, "Junaluska."

56. Quoted in Gilbert, *The Trail of Tears Across Missouri,* p. 46.

Chapter Five: Starting Over

57. William G. McLoughlin, *After the Trail of Tears: The Cherokee Struggle for Sovereignty, 1839–1880.* Chapel Hill: University of North Carolina Press, 1993, p. 5.

58. Quoted in McLoughlin, *After the Trail of Tears,* p. 5.

59. Quoted in McLoughlin, *After the Trail of Tears,* p. 10.

60. Quoted in Emmet Starr, *History of the Cherokee Indians and Their Legends and Folk Lore.* Oklahoma City: Warden, 1921, p. 112.

61. Quoted in Ehle, *Trail of Tears,* p. 371.

62. Quoted in About North Georgia, "Major Ridge."

63. McLoughlin, *After the Trail of Tears,* p. 16.

64. Quoted in McLoughlin, *After the Trail of Tears,* pp. 19–20.

65. Quoted in McLoughlin, *After the Trail of Tears,* p. 35.

66. Quoted in Albert Bender, "Walking in the Footsteps of Our Ancestors," News from Indian Country. http:// indiancountrynews.net/index .php?option=com_content&task=vie w&id=6840&Itemid=1.

67. Quoted in Perdue and Green, *The Cherokee Removal,* p. 186.

68. The Cherokee Nation, "A Brief History of the Cherokee Nation." www .cherokee.org/Culture/57/Page/de fault.aspx.

For Further Research

Books

Alex W. Bealer, *Only the Names Remain: The Cherokee and the Trail of Tears.* New York: Little, Brown, 1996. Originally written in 1976, this illustrated version provides a dramatic account of the Cherokees' journey through bitter cold and blazing heat.

D.L. Birchfield, *The Trail of Tears.* Milwaukee: World Almanac Library, 2003. A short, easy-to-read account of the forced relocation of the Cherokee Nation.

John P. Bowes, *The Trail of Tears: Removal in the South.* New York: Chelsea House, 2007. This insightful, easy-to-read book broadens the story of the Trail of Tears to include the story of the removal of all of the "Five Civilized Tribes" from the southeastern United States.

Ann Byers, *The Trail of Tears: A Primary Source History of the Forced Relocation of the Cherokee Nation.* New York: Rosen, 2004. Ample illustrations and primary source materials accompany the text and help readers understand the causes and effects of U.S. relocation policies that forced the Cherokees from their homeland in the southeast.

Joan Gilbert, *The Trail of Tears Across Missouri.* Columbia: University of Missouri Press, 1996. This easy reader, appropriate for young teens and adults alike, describes the causes of the forced relocation of the Cherokees and tells the tragic story of their travails as they traveled from the southeastern United States to the land set aside for them in present-day Oklahoma.

Duane H. King, *The Cherokee Trail of Tears.* Portland: Graphic Arts Center, 2008. This book draws heavily upon diaries, newspaper accounts, nineteenth-century maps, oral traditions, and more to re-create the journey of the Cherokees from their homeland in the southeast to Indian Territory. The text is accompanied by inset sections of full-color photographs by photographer David G. Fitzgerald.

Katie Marsico, *Trail of Tears: The Tragedy of American Indians.* New York: Benchmark, 2009. This comprehensive account of the forced removal of American Indians from their homes in the east to the Oklahoma Territory includes substantial information on the Cherokee people and their legacy.

Theda Perdue and Michael D. Green, *The Cherokee Nation and the Trail of Tears.* New York: Viking Adult, 2007. This account follows the Cherokees from before European contact to their forced expulsion from the southern Appalachians to the new Indian Territory, with emphasis on the U.S. policies that resulted in their removal. Although written for an adult audience, the engaging style of the authors makes it accessible to students as well.

Theda Perdue and Michael D. Green, *The Cherokee Removal: A Brief History with Documents*. Boston: Bedford/St. Martin's, 2005. Written by historians and experts on Cherokee history, this book provides documents, letters, memoirs, and other primary source materials, accompanied by a historical narrative and suggestions for how to interpret and/or analyze the documents.

Vicki Rozema, *Voices from the Trail of Tears*. New York: John F. Blair, 2003. This collection of first-person accounts of the Cherokee removal of 1838 includes letters, journals, military reports, contemporary newspaper accounts, doctors' reports, and other primary source materials.

Elliott West, *Trail of Tears National Historic Trail*. Tucson: Southwest Parks and Monuments Association, 2000. This beautifully illustrated book tells of the travails along the routes taken by the Cherokees and other Native Americans removed from the southeastern United States during the 1830s.

Internet Sources

The Cherokee Nation, "A Brief History of the Trail of Tears," 1998–2002. www.cherokee.org/Culture/58/Page/default.aspx.

Randy Golden, "Cherokee Removal Forts," About North Georgia, 1997. http://ngeorgia.com/history/cherokeeforts.html.

Randy Golden, "The Trail of Tears," About North Georgia. http://ngeorgia.com/history/nghisttt.html.

Randy Golden, "The Trail of Tears," Our Georgia History. http://ourgeorgiahistory.com/indians/cherokee/trail_of_tears.html.

PBS Online, "Indian Removal." www.pbs.org/wgbh/aia/part4/4p2959.html.

Web Sites

American Native Press Archives, Sequoyah Research Center (www.anpa.ualr.edu). This Web site, part of the University of Arkansas, Little Rock, maintains a comprehensive collection of Native American newspapers, periodicals, and other publications. Several pages are devoted to the Trail of Tears, providing eyewitness accounts, letters, maps, site reports, and a host of other resources.

The Cherokee Nation (www.cherokee.org). The Cherokee Nation's Internet library of information on the Trail of Tears includes primary source materials and firsthand accounts. The Web site also provides information on the culture and history of the Cherokee Nation before and after the Trail of Tears and on the government, population, events, and other aspects of Cherokee life today.

The *Cherokee Phoenix* from Hunter Library (www.wcu.edu/library/CherokeePhoenix). This Web site gives a brief overview of the *Cherokee Phoenix*, which was published from 1828 to 1834, and offers a searchable database of the articles published in this newspaper.

History of the Cherokee (http://cherokeehistory.com). Designed and maintained by Ken Martin, a Cherokee of mixed blood and a tribal member of the Cherokee Nation of Oklahoma, this Web site provides a factual account of Cherokee history before, during, and after the Trail of Tears as well as images and maps, books and newspapers, and links to other resources.

Indian Affairs: Laws and Treaties (http://digital.library.okstate.edu/kappler/index.htm). This is a comprehensive compilation of U.S. treaties, laws, and executive orders pertaining to Native American tribes. The information was originally compiled and edited by Charles K. Kappler in 1904. Due to their historic significance, the seven volumes compiled in 1904 were converted to a digital format and indexed for use by researchers.

National Park Service, Trail of Tears National Historic Trail (www.nps.gov/trte). This Web site provides information and stories about the routes taken as the Native Americans traveled westward and the culture and history of the Native Americans today.

Index

A
Act of Union (1839), 82
Adair, James, 22
American Revolution, 28
Arbuckle, Matthew, 82
Arkansas Gazette (newspaper), 71

B
Battle of Horseshoe Bend, 75
Boudinot, Elias, 45, 53, 79
Brown, John, 78
Bushyhead, Jack, 77
Bushyhead, Jesse, 75, 92
Butler, Elizur, 75

C
Cannon, B.B., 53
Cherokee Advocate (newspaper), 83–84
Cherokee Constitution, 36, 37–38
Cherokee Council, 37
Cherokee Nation v. Georgia (1831), 42
Cherokee National Historical Society, 91
Cherokee Phoenix (newspaper), 28, 35, 50
Cherokee rose, 71
Cherokees/Cherokee Nation
  alliances with colonial governments, 24
  alphabet of, *34*
  in American Revolution, 28
  assimilation into white society, 33–34
  assimilation policy and, 29–30
  current status of, 86–88
  daily life of, 14–18
  1835 census of, 52
  first contact with Europeans, 14, *15*
  in French and Indian War, 25–26
  on Indian Removal Act, 44
  movement to lands west of Mississippi, 46
  origin of name, 14
  schism between Treaty Party and National Party of, 46–49
Chickamaugas, 27, 28–29
Civil War (1861–1865), 85
Clay, Henry, 39
Clinton, Bill, 91
Costner, Kevin, 91
Crockett, Davy, 39–40
Cuming, Alexander, 24, *25*
Cyrus, Miley, 91

D
De Soto, Hernando, 14
Deas, Edward, 72
Depp, Johnny, 91
Disease, 22, 24
Dwellings, 14–15, *16*

E
Eastern Band of Cherokees, 59, 86–87, 87–88

1838 Removal, 60–62
  under Cherokee leadership, 64–66
  official numbers of, *64*
  See also Trail of Tears
Ellis, Jerry, 92
Emerson, Ralph Waldo, 52

F
Fort Cass (TN), 58
French and Indian War (1754–1763),
  25, *26*

G
Georgia
  agreement between federal
    government and, 32–33
  removal of Cherokees from, 56–58
  tensions between Cherokees and
    whites in, 38–39
Georgia, Cherokee Nation v. (1831), 42
Georgia, Worcester v. (1832), 42–43
Gilbert, Joan, 29–30
Gold, 38
Green, Michael D., 21

H
Henderson Purchase (1775), 27
Hendrix, Jimi, 91
Hicks, George, 72
Hildebrand, Louis, 92
Hildebrand, Nancy Bushyhead
  Walker, 92

I
Indian Removal Act (1830), 10, 36,
  41
  Cherokee Nation's objection to, 44
  Relocation Districts under, *40*
Indian Territory
  challenges of life in, 76

Cherokees build new society in,
  83–85
clashes between whites and
  Cherokee in, 77–79
creation of, 10
encroachment of white settlers
  into, 85–86
first detachment of Cherokees set
  out for, 60–62
Native American tribes relocated
  to, 13
removal routes to, *63*
Indian Trade and Intercourse Act
  (1789), 31

J
Jackson, Andrew, 10, 33, 75
  Indian policy of, 41
  as proponent of Indian removal, 40
  on verdict in *Worcester v. State of
    Georgia*, 43
  view on removal of Indians, 35–36,
    44
Jefferson, Thomas, 32
Jones, Evan, 56, 58, 69
Junaluska (Tsunu'lahun'ski), 75

K
Know, Henry, 29

L
Lynn, Loretta, 91

M
Mankiller, Wilma, 88–89
Marshall, John, 42, 43
McLoughlin, William G., 77–78, 81

N
National Park Service, 92

National Party (Ross Party),
  48–49
Native American tribes
  colonial governments' alliances
    with, 24
  in eastern U.S., 12
  federal government given
    authority over, 29, 31–32
Native Americans
  lands given up by, 63
  whites' view of as inferior, 35

O
Oklahoma, 86

P
Perdue, Theda, 21

R
Ridge, John, 47, 79, 80
Ridge, Major, 47, 48, 49, 79
  on reasons for signing Treaty of
    New Echota, 50
Rogers, Will, 91
Ross, Andrew, 47
Ross, John, 47, 75, 83
  appeals to Washington by, 39,
    44–45
  forms alliance with Confederacy,
    85
  as leader of Cherokee Nation,
    48
  as member of removal committee,
    62
  protests Treaty of New Echota,
    50–51
  retaliation against Treaty Party
    and, 81–82
  on Treaty of New Echota, 51
Ross, Quatie, 75

S
Schermerhorn, John F., 49, 79, 81
Scott, Winfield, 55–56, 56, 58, 62
  on Cherokee people, 69
Sequoyah, 33, 35
Smith, Chadwick "Corntassel," 81
St. Louis Post-Dispatch (newspaper),
  77
Stokes, Montfort, 78
Supreme Court, 32

T
Talking the Trail (Ellis), 92
Trail of Tears
  commemorations of, 11, 89, 90,
    91–92
  death toll from, 11, 13
  escapees from, 72–73, 75
  help/hindrances by whites along,
    71–72
  life on, 66, 68–71
  route, 63
  See also 1838 Removal
The Trail of Tears Across Missouri
  (Gilbert), 29–30
Trail of Tears State Park (MO), 92
Treaty of Holston (1791), 29
Treaty of Hopewell (1785), 29
Treaty of New Echota (1835), 49, 73,
  79
  fate of signers of, 79
  Major Ridge on reasons for
    signing, 50
  protests against, 50–51
  See also Treaty Party
Treaty of Paris (1763), 25
Treaty Party, 47–48, 85
  conflict between National Party
    and, 49, 50–51
  defense of, 53

trial/killings of leaders of, 79,
  81–82
Tsali, 57
Tuscarora tribe, 24

U
United Keetoowah Band, 86
U.S. Constitution, 29, 31, 42

V
Van Buren, Martin, 52

Villages, Native American, *17*
  life in, 18, 20–21

W
War Department, U.S., 42
Washington, George, 27, 29
Watie, Stand, 73, 83
Webster, Daniel, 39
Wool, John E., 52–53
Worcester v. State of Georgia (1832),
  42–43

Picture Credits

About the Author

Lydia Bjornlund is a freelance writer in northern Virginia, where she lives with her husband, Gerry Hoetmer, and their wonderful children, Jake and Sophia. She has written more than a dozen nonfiction books for children, mostly on American history and health-related topics. She also writes books and training materials for adults on land conservation, the environment, public management, and other issues. Bjornlund holds a master's degree in education from Harvard University and a bachelor's degree from Williams College.